PRAI

for *The Advisor Breakthrough*
and Shawn Sparks

"Shawn is the Advisor's Advisor! Not many coaches can say they helped their advisors raise over $5 billion of new assets. If you want hyper growth with more fun, more time, and more money, this is a must read!"

—**Josh Mellberg,** founder and CEO of JD Mellberg, host of PBS retirement planning program, *Mastering Your Money,* and featured guest on Yahoo! and CNBC

"Very few people have the access to so many top financial advisors. Even fewer use that access to build a step-by-step guide on how to achieve incredible success and break through as an advisor. Shawn has both. He has used the relationships he's built and the knowledge those relationships have brought him and condensed it into a single book that shows every advisor the "secrets" to success in this business. If you read this book and implement the ideas Shawn shares, you are sure to find success."

—**Cody Foster,** co-founder of Advisors Excel, one of the country's fastest-growing insurance marketing organizations (IMO)

"Success leaves clues, and there's no better sleuth than Shawn when it comes to discovering what an advisor needs to become and stay successful. He has worked and coached some of the most elite financial advisors in the country, and with this privileged access, he has been able to distill all of the necessary ingredients into this book to be an ultra-successful, high-demand financial advisor and stand out among the masses. No matter where you're at in your journey, this book is a must!"

—**Rob Russell,** president of Russell & Company, featured *Forbes* contributor and co-host of *Retirement Rescue Radio*

"I started working with Shawn in 2010 and, since then, our revenues have grown four fold and profits eight fold. He has been a great resource to me as I have led my firm through a massive growth phase. We would not be where we are without partners like Shawn. He has had a great impact on our company, our twenty-four employees, and their clients. If you are a financial advisor or own a financial services firm, Shawn is the real deal to help you get to the next level."

—**Joel M. Johnson,** CFP, Johnson Brunetti
& JB Capital, host of the *Money Wisdom* radio
program and frequent contributor to *Forbes*

"Shawn Sparks has spent a decade helping the country's top financial advisors grow their businesses and make a bigger impact for their clients. In this book, Shawn distills the best of what he has seen proven to create market dominance for those in the financial services industry. Read this book if that is your goal, but keep it hidden from your competition."

—**Darren Hardy,** *New York Times* best-selling
author of *The Compound Effect* and former publisher
and founding editor *SUCCESS Magazine*

THE
ADVISOR
BREAKTHROUGH

THE
ADVISOR
BREAKTHROUGH

YOUR STEP-BY-STEP GUIDE TO BUILDING A MILLION-DOLLAR PRACTICE

SHAWN SPARKS

ELITE
PERFORMANCE
PUBLISHING

This publication is designed to provide general information regarding the subject matter covered. However, laws and practices often vary from state to state and are subject to change. Be sure to review and understand the laws and regulations in each state in which you conduct business.

This book has been written to assist financial advisors (herein referred to as "advisors") who are properly registered with a fee-based Registered Investment Advisory firm. Individuals who are not registered as such may not offer financial planning or advisory services, or provide specific advice to consumers on investments and/or financial plans.

This book includes a number of suggestions for ways that advisors can provide clients and prospects with certain benefits, such as nominal gifts, meals, or forms of entertainment. Keep in mind that state insurance departments often have regulations that outline what types of gifts (including dollar amount thresholds) insurance professionals can give to consumers. In addition, your broker/dealer or Registered Investment Advisor may also have gifting limits for consumers which you should be familiar with. To protect your practice, be sure to understand and follow all rebating and gifting laws in the states in which you conduct business.

The author and publisher have taken reasonable precautions in the preparation of this book and believe the facts presented within are accurate as of the date it was written. However, neither the author nor the publisher assumes any responsibility for any errors or omissions. The author and publisher specifically disclaim any liability resulting from the use or application of the information contained in this book, and the information is not intended to serve as legal, financial, or other professional advice related to individual situations.

Published by Elite Performance Publishing, Lawrence, KS.

Cover design and composition by Accelerate Media Partners, LLC

Copy editing by The Media Concierge, LLC

Hardcover ISBN 13: 978-0-9979640-0-4

Paperback ISBN 13: 978-0-9979640-1-1

LCCN: 2016951423

Printed in the United States of America

To the advisors I've worked with over the years.

You've taught me that true success has nothing to do with money and everything to do with the difference you can make in the lives of others.

For that, I am forever grateful.

ACKNOWLEDGMENTS

One of life's greatest blessings is finding something you love to do for a living. An even greater blessing is doing that something with people you also love working with.

The Advisor Breakthrough was written for, and inspired by, the many advisors I've had the fortune to work with over the last ten years. Not only have I learned something from each of these advisors, many went out of their way to help me. They shared lessons that allowed me to grow both professionally and personally. Some of these incredible lessons we learned together, others we learned independently. All of these lessons not only shaped my career, they also blessed my life.

I believe in the power of association, and my associations are what made *The Advisor Breakthrough* possible. The successful, thoughtful people I've worked with in this business have rubbed off on me and influenced who I have become. These advisors are not just great advisors, they are also extraordinary people. I'm lucky to consider them among my friends and am forever indebted to them.

While I can't possibly thank everyone by name, I'd like to first thank God for giving me the gifts that he has and allowing me to use those gifts in a platform where I can serve others. I'd also like to thank my wonderful wife Aubrey and our daughters Sadie and AnnMarie, for their love and support and allowing me to spend many nights and weekends working on this book. I'd like to thank my parents, for not just telling me how to live but showing me how to live at the same time. I'd like to thank my twin brother Ryan, who has always been, and will always be my best friend.

The three owners of Advisors Excel—Dave Callanan, Derek Thompson, and Cody Foster—have been tremendous mentors, and I greatly appreciate their guidance throughout the years.

I have also been fortunate to work with an incredible team at Advisors Excel. I am reminded daily not only of the incredible support and insights they provide within Advisors Excel, but also of what an incredible asset they are to each of the advisors they serve. They are truly the best in the business.

I have really struggled with how to thank and acknowledge the many advisors who collectively contributed to the wisdom within these pages. There are simply too many to mention by name, but each of you know who you are. Please know that I thank each and every one of you from my heart.

Lastly, I would like to thank Reed Bilbray, Ivy Hughes, and Erica Jennings for bringing this book to life. You've all been a real pleasure to work with.

CONTENTS

FOREWORD

One of my favorite sayings–it actually hangs on the wall of my office–is "Success leaves clues, and the successful are always in search of them."

There's a reason why *The Advisor Breakthrough* is special and why you should dive deeply into its contents: it is loaded with the clues from the most successful.

Shawn Sparks has worked with thousands of advisors over the last decade. He has seen the haves and the have nots. He has watched as advisors grew their businesses tenfold, and he has watched others who seemingly have the same opportunities plateau or even fail completely. He has seen every combination of success/failure that you can imagine…and he has done that thing that makes him so valuable: He has taken notes on all of it.

In those notes, Shawn has found answers to the questions everyone wants to ask: Why do some fail? Why do others succeed? What key factors lead to growth? What are the challenges that may lead an advisor to struggle?

The Advisor Breakthrough is unique. I believe that nowhere else on the market will you find such a comprehensive guide to building a multi-million dollar advisory practice. *The Advisor Breakthrough* will become the to go-to resource for every financial advisor who wants to land among the industry's top one percent.

Let's be honest, one of the greatest challenges of entrepreneurship is finding someone credible that we can engage, someone to whom we can comfortably admit our limitations, and whose experiences can help us grow. That's where Shawn's unique access to the best in class comes to your rescue. He has asked those questions you would have asked if given the chance, and he brings the answers to you in *Breakthrough*.

As Shawn shared his goals for this project with me, he kept coming back to one theme: build a book that shortens the learning curve for those who want to grow and build their practices. As you'll read here, he has certainly succeeded.

Some of the best takeaways from *The Advisor Breakthrough* include:

1. You can build the advisory practice of your dreams. You have what it takes, but in order to do this, you have to be clear about what you want and *why* you want it. You then have to be on a quest for knowledge and work relentlessly to pursue it.

2. The financial advisory business is really all about helping people. The better you build your business, the more people you can help. The best advisors don't think about their own financial gain. Instead, they focus on helping people. The byproduct is that they find more success.

3. Sometimes advisors make this business a lot more complex than it really is. But this business is simple. It's three businesses in one: marketing, sales, and operations. Think of this business as a stool. If one leg is rickety, the whole thing will go over.

4. No individual can accomplish as much as a great team can. Building a great team and taking great care of them will be a huge factor in your success.

5. If you want to land among the top one percent of financial advisors, you have to constantly overdeliver. Give every one of your clients an incredible experience. Offer them value at every turn, and before you know it, they'll become raving fans. Those raving fans will then bring more clients who are just like them, to you.

If you believe as I do that "success leaves clues," read *Breakthrough* because Shawn doesn't leave a single page without one.

Follow these clues, and you will attain whatever level of success you set for yourself.

Don Yaeger
Nine-time *New York Times* best-selling author
Great Teams: 16 Things High-Performing
Organizations Do Differently

INTRODUCTION

"In this business, you can make all the money in the world. But if you do it for the money, you won't make a penny. If you do it for the people, you will never have to worry about the money."

— *Elite Advisor, MN*[1]

I think of myself as a connector. I connect resources, ideas, people, and information to financial advisors so they can break through mediocrity and build the business of their dreams. I've been studying and working with financial advisors for more than a decade, and everything I learn from each advisor—be it a key piece of information or a groundbreaking idea—I share with another.

As vice president of advisor development for Advisors Excel, I have studied successful financial advisors with decades of experience for more than ten years and can tell you there isn't a single thing they do that you can't learn to do, too. No matter how you came into the financial advisory business, if you follow the lessons in *Breakthrough*, you can develop the business of your dreams.

---

1 To protect the privacy of my advisors, I have withheld their names. Many of the stories in this book come from individual advisors with whom I have worked; however, some of the stories combine the experiences of several advisors into a single story to clarify and strengthen a point.

There are more than 300,000 financial advisors in the United States. I work with 150 of the most successful ones. They work as much as the rest of us, but they accomplish so much more. Overall, they make an average of $400,000 a year. This is significantly higher than the 2013 median income for a financial advisor, which was $75,320[2].

I have worked with advisors who love every minute of their workweek. I have also worked with advisors who can't stand going into the office. I have watched advisors create businesses that support their lifestyle, and I have watched advisors become slaves to their businesses. I have worked with the haves *and* the have-nots. I have investigated what it takes to become successful and have spent thousands of hours learning from thousands of elite advisors. I'm blessed because today, I have the chance to share that expertise with you.

I am passionate about helping people. The best way for me to do that is to teach you the skills you can develop to help yourself. Know that you are in control of your own destiny and you *can* accomplish your goals in this business. Why not use the top lessons from the country's most successful advisors to reach those goals more quickly?

I came to this industry because of my dad, who has worked in financial services for more than thirty years. I was much more interested in how dad affected people than I was in what he did for a living. Every time I showed up to his office, he was positively impacting someone—a kid from school, another business owner, or a community member. This ability to help other people on a grand scale was captivating, so I followed in dad's footsteps and studied finance at Kansas State University (KSU). Six months before I graduated, I interviewed with a few financial firms. They asked if I could go six months without a paycheck. I couldn't. Just as I was getting discouraged, dad asked if I'd ever heard of insurance marketing organizations (IMO).

I had no idea what dad was talking about, but applied for a marketing job with Personalized Brokerage Service (PBS). Although

---

2 http://learn.org/articles/Financial_Advisor_Salary_and_Career_FAQs.html

the job offer wasn't for a financial advisor, I took it because it involved helping successful financial advisors grow their businesses. I viewed the job as an opportunity to learn from highly successful people who were doing what I wanted to do.

Early on in my career, I decided to learn something from every advisor I talked to. I asked questions no one else asked, jotted down ideas and thoughts, and went to the bookstore at the end of every day to do more research. I told myself, "If I'm going to work with advisors, I need to talk like them." I need to understand industry jargon, financial information, and anything else that could come up during client interactions. I was a sponge, which allowed me to develop a knowledge base that was really helpful to the advisors I worked with.

Not long after, I had my aha moment. I was talking to an advisor who had an issue with his business. The issue he was dealing with was *exactly* the same issue another advisor had solved the day before. I shared the advice with the first advisor, who was absolutely thrilled to hear how another advisor solved the same problem. I found that my advice, which came directly from another advisor, made all the difference. It was the key ingredient the advisor who was struggling needed to take his business to the next level!

That day, I realized the best way I could help my advisors was by becoming a connector and sharing what I learned from them with other advisors. An advisor shares one idea with me, and immediately gets fifty ideas from other advisors who have shared solutions to those problems with me. I was the connection that made that possible.

A short time later, I realized my new mission to help advisors grow their business was unique among my peers and the company I worked for. Most of the people I was surrounded by pushed products and targeted a mass audience of advisors hoping that a few might stick. The model was all about bringing in whomever, whenever and not at all about connecting to the advisors, getting to know them as people, helping them grow, and bringing them value.

I was expected to call and bring on thousands of advisors. I was paid a huge bonus one month for recruiting more than fifty advisors. It was good because I got paid, but as far as I saw it, it was meaningless for the growth of the company because I then had to work with fifty advisors who were a waste of my time. For example, I once licensed an eighty-year-old advisor who no longer wrote business, but kept his license current just in case a friend needed help. I got paid for licensing the guy, yet it didn't matter if he wrote business or not.

I quickly found that the advisors who wanted all the time and attention were the ones who weren't producing. The ones who were successful didn't have the time to sit and just chat. This model created a lot of demands on my time and yet produced little. When one of my top advisors needed me, I wasn't available because I was working with an advisor who wasn't ideal for me. This business model wasn't a recipe for success, which is how I found Advisors Excel.

I'll remember that first meeting with Advisors Excel for the rest of my life. I told the owners it seemed meaningless that my manager was looking over my shoulder making sure I called the 2,000 advisors I was supposed to be working with when I really only wanted to focus on my top 1 percent as 90 percent of my income came from them. When they told me they only wanted me working with the top 1 percent, I became Advisors Excel's ninth employee.

That's when I really started to learn. The quality of ideas coming from the Advisors Excel advisors was incredible. The higher quality of ideas I received, the more I learned, and the better I was able to help my advisors.

I have now spent more than ten years learning about the unusual and impressive skills that separate elite advisors from the rest, the enormity of their successes and failures, and their shortcomings, which tend to come from their biggest strengths. I've asked questions that unveil how an advisor triples their business in twelve months. I've witnessed advisors hit a plateau and then a decline in production during the same twelve months. I've seen it, lived it, helped diagnose what went wrong, and provided insights into how they can succeed.

As a financial advisor, I could have helped maybe one hundred people a year. Working with financial advisors as part of one of the country's leading IMOs, I help 10,000 people a year. My one hundred advisors help one hundred people a year, so together, we help 10,000 people. I love that by helping advisors run a better business, they're able to help more people.

Every advisor wants the perfect practice. They want a practice that rewards them with more time, more fun, and more money. They want to know they're having a positive impact on their clients, and they want to own a business rather than have a business that owns them. They want the ultimate advisory practice, one where they spend each day doing the things they enjoy, rather than spending each day managing chaos.

Unfortunately, what advisors want and what they have is miles apart. Instead of the ultimate practice, most advisors have a lonely practice. They don't feel they have what it takes to reach the level of success they dream about. It doesn't have to be that way. You *can* build the business you want—one that will not become your life— but one that will *bless* your life.

Take the lessons in *Breakthrough* and achieve profound and sustainable growth. Don't look at that imaginary glass ceiling that's holding you back and wonder *why* you've plateaued. Take a hammer and bust through it! Learn to attract the right clients so you are no longer the best-kept secret in your market, and build a better business for you, your clients, and your family.

Instead of relying on your own experience, let's tap into the minds of the most successful advisors who work with Advisors Excel—the elite—and see what it takes to break through mediocrity. As you'll see in *Breakthrough*, top advisors share a similar set of habits, processes, and outlooks. The intent of this book is to help you decipher these habits and immediately put them to work so you can shortcut your journey to success.

Let's get serious about marketing. Let's get serious about selling. Let's get serious about operations, and let's get serious about helping people. Let's get serious about building a practice you run rather than building one that runs you.

How to Best Make *The Advisor Breakthrough* Work for You

You're not reading *The Advisor Breakthrough* because you want to be a *good* advisor. You're reading it because you want to be an *elite* advisor.

One thing you'll learn in *The Advisor Breakthrough* is that elite advisors never reinvent the wheel. They learn everything they can from people who have already had enormous success, and then they implement those lessons immediately in their own businesses.

Because I want you to be the best, I've developed a GO Elite Advisor Action Plan. The GO Elite Advisor Action Plan includes several Go Elite items at the end of every chapter. This plan takes the key points of every chapter and turns them into actionable items you can implement *today* to build your ultimate practice.

By the time you finish *The Advisor Breakthrough*, you will have ninety-five small actions that will change your business. Your business wasn't built in a day. There isn't one single big thing you can do to change it. You must do ninety-five little things to build that business you've always dreamed of.

Now, get a cup of coffee and a notepad, and let's get to work!

SECTION I
MASTER
THE GAME

"True wisdom is learning something from everybody."

— Elite Advisor, IL

Every financial professional wants to be a top producer, yet very few are. If you want the freedom, enjoyment, and flexibility top advisors have, quit relying on lessons learned from your own experiences, and start learning from those of top producers. Take what I've learned from working with the country's top advisors during the last ten years, and focus on people instead of money, action instead of talk, and greatness instead of the status quo.

While their approaches to marketing and adding clients may differ, high-caliber advisors know what they want and why they want it, and they pursue both relentlessly. They understand mental focus is the number one factor separating mediocrity from greatness. The game is 90 percent mental. Success requires consistency and perseverance.

This business is tough. In fact, an overwhelming statistic proves the majority of financial advisors working in the United States not only fail to reach a high level of success, they fail period. They fail to work hard and smart, they fail to understand success is 100 percent within their control, and they fail to focus on the right things.

This business is full of ups and downs. One week you have a calendar full of appointments and make a lot of revenue. The next, it's just you in an office counting minutes, feeling like a failure because you haven't had a single appointment or conversation with a prospect. Elite advisors have off days too, but they also have the confidence to keep going when it's tough. They have the ideas, resources, information, inspiration, and collective wisdom to manage the natural ebbs and flows of business. They are masters of their game.

The good news is, those who have mastered the game don't belong to an exclusive club. I've watched people just like you hit goals they never dreamed possible by simply changing their thought process. Your potential directly relates to the way you think.

When I was struggling to tackle a challenge, one of my top advisors said, "Shawn, you aren't thinking big enough."

As you read *Breakthrough*, you'll realize that you, too, aren't thinking big enough. When you finish, you, too, will start thinking big.

I've watched people just like you hit
goals they never dreamed possible
by simply changing their thought
process. Your potential directly
relates to the way you think.

Elite advisors understand that thinking small and accepting
mediocrity leads to small success. They know those who think big
are unstoppable. *Breakthrough* will help you think big. *Breakthrough*
will make you unstoppable.

OBJECTIVES

Section 1: Master the Game

In this section, you will learn how to:

- Define *what* you want from your business and *why* you want it
- Develop strong work habits
- Set daily goals that will help you meet your annual goals
- Implement great ideas within 72 hours
- Connect to and learn from other successful people

1

KNOW WHAT YOU WANT

"Whatever the mind can conceive
and believe, it can achieve."

—*Napoleon Hill*

You won't get anywhere in this business if you don't have a clear picture of where you're going. Advisors with outstanding production know something you don't: their production is the result of their dreams. Before we talk hard work, motivation, behavior, and activity, let's define what you're after.

Clear your mind for a minute, grab a pen, and answer this question honestly: "What do I want from my business?"

1) _____

2) _____

3) _____

Does your answer involve a number? New assets sold, revenue earned, or clients added? If the answer is yes, you're not alone. There's a misnomer in the business world that knowing what you want from your business directly correlates to financial outcomes.

Key performance indicators (KPIs) weighing financial success, such as earnings per share and sales growth, are used by companies around the world to measure success. There's one big problem with this approach. Money only tells a fraction of the story, and KPIs often lead to an endless cycle of less-fulfilling outcomes.

Reenvision What Success Means to You

Knowing what you want isn't just about productivity in terms of dollars and cents. It's about creating the business you want and doing more with the gifts you already have. It's about developing a fulfilling business that will sustain you when things go wrong. It's about developing a mission that extends beyond finance because— and I hate to be the bearer of this message—contrary to what we've been told, *money isn't a sustainable motivator.*

Unlike average advisors, elite advisors consider personal goals, time management, and quality of life when defining what they want. They seek a business they own, rather than one that owns them.

Take Advisor's Excel advisor Dave, who called after he clipped $20 million in assets, which was a huge accomplishment. He said, "Shawn, I'm going to write $40 million next year."

Since Dave and I were thinking about traditional finance-based productivity as the only benchmark for success, I was really impressed and encouraged Dave to go for it. Interestingly, I shared the conversation with another advisor, Jeff, who had been bringing in $40 million in new assets per year for the last five years. Jeff suggested we were moving too fast and looking at productivity through too narrow of a lens.

Jeff said, "Would Dave rather do $40 million a year or $20 million again in half the amount of time worked every week?"

This is why elite advisors are so great. They bring a perspective that makes us think differently. A guy who had been consistently on top for more than five years shared his view and forced us to think differently about growth. At one point in time, Jeff had asked himself the same question. What did he want from his business? It turns out he wanted a business that blessed his life. Once Jeff defined what he wanted, he found his motivator.

Build a Business You Own, Not One that Owns You

Think about this. Is it better to work twenty-five hours a week for $20 million? Or fifty hours a week for $40 million?

Both Dave and Jeff are incredible businessmen, but their definitions of productivity and success differ, which impacts how they run their businesses. Jeff wants a lifestyle business that provides a good living, but requires fewer hours and allows him to pursue other interests. Dave thinks he wants to maximize financial output. Neither approach is wrong. There is no right answer when it comes to determining what you want from your business, and those desires may change over time. Whether you want an income-based or lifestyle-based business, the clearer you are in what you want, the easier it is to achieve.

Whether you pursue a twenty-five-hour workweek or forty-hour workweek, $200,000 in revenue or $20 million, money isn't the only way to define what you want from your business. Growth is really about advancing your business to where you want it to be by developing and creating a vision that works for you.

Growth is really about progressing your business to where you want it to be by developing and creating a vision that works for you.

Once you create the vision you want for your business, it will drive everything you do. It will dictate the infrastructure, your budget, the decisions you make, and the team you create. Every person on your team must buy into that vision, pursue it relentlessly, and accept the mindset that failure is not an option. Never let that vision go.

Everyone wants to grow, but too many people aren't willing to make the necessary changes to realize their vision. You've got to be willing to adjust your business for your vision to become a reality.

> Everyone wants to grow, but too many people aren't willing to make the necessary changes to realize their vision.

For example, I have an advisor who feels meeting with clients isn't really his strength, but he loves marketing and building his business. He built a vision and business where he does all the marketing and his associates meet with clients. For him, his vision was to build a business where he focused on marketing strategies, not meeting with clients.

Another advisor I worked with retired from a sixty-hour-a-week job at a very young age. He had more time than he knew what to do with, which was great until he realized none of his friends were retired. When he wanted to golf, he didn't have anyone to golf with. Retirement wasn't what he thought it would be, so he started a new career as a financial advisor. He knew finance, wanted to help people, and needed to stay busy. His second career resulted in a $350,000-a-year paycheck, yet he only worked twenty-five hours a week. He called it, semi-retirement, or a hybrid of working and relaxation. He wanted a business that didn't run his life. He molded his business into the business he wanted. You can do that, too.

Design a Business that Fuels Your Life

Many of the advisors I work with hit a wall or burn out after pursuing standard industry definitions of growth. They may achieve remarkable financial goals, but feel flat, defeated, and depressed after reaching those milestones. They just go with the flow without knowing where they're headed. That isn't victory. Victory is making real progress toward what you really want. The more clearly you define what you want—the closer you stick to your vision—the happier you'll be with your accomplishments.

Let's get that pen again. This time, challenge yourself and rethink your idea of success. What do you truly want? Money? A multimillion dollar business? A business that's fulfilling, but includes lots of free time for a nice work/family balance? A twenty-hour workweek?

Your answers will help define your business and vision. They will also provide a framework for building a practice that brings more meaning to your life, rather than building a practice that owns you.

Chapter 1: Know What You Want

Paint a clear picture of your ideal business by:

1) Clearly defining what rewards you want from your business

2) Developing a vision around those rewards

3) Sharing that vision with your team

2

SEPARATE THE MISSION FROM THE COMMISSION

"Success is not the key to happiness.
Happiness is the key to success. If you
love what you do, you will find success."

—*Albert Schweitzer*

This business is pretty simple. You have to bring prospects in, convert them to clients, and keep them happy by maintaining the relationship. In other words, marketing, sales, operations. That being said, how you connect to people and how that connection impacts others will have far more impact on your success than marketing, sales, and operations alone.

In this business, we have the commission—or the cash—and the mission, which is the heart of what we do. While the commission is nice, it's the mission that keeps the blood pumping. It takes a mature, grounded person to separate the two and focus on the mission. Elite advisors tend to focus more on the mission than on the commission. The majority of advisors do not. They're too busy chasing the money—chasing what's in it for them—instead of focusing on helping the client.

Develop a Mission, Skyrocket Your Commission

To separate the mission from the commission, helping people must be your focus. Great advisors realize the huge responsibility that comes with investing other people's hard-earned money. They don't look at prospects as profit. They view prospects as people to help. They understand that their clients' investments represent a lifetime of hard work and that the success of their business depends on helping others secure a sustainable financial future. The mission is to do right by the client. If that isn't at the forefront of your mind, you're in the wrong business, and your long-term success will be limited.

Zig Ziglar said, "You can have everything in life you want, if you'll just help enough other people get what they want."

Live by that. Success comes more easily when you focus on how you can benefit those you serve. It's also important to understand your personal mission. Why are you in this? Whether growth is defined by $600,000 in revenue, four staff, or a twenty-hour workweek, it's critical to identify the underlying motivation for achieving your personal goals. You have to know *why* you want to grow, why you do what you do, and what the real purpose is that you see for your life.

Let me explain. A few years ago, one Advisor Excel advisor—I'll call him Robert—told me a story about a couple who came into his office. They wanted some retirement advice. Robert put together an income plan for them and said that if they wanted to retire, they could. They were shocked. The husband had worked all his life and hadn't realized retirement was an option. He was astounded to discover they were going to be okay and made the decision to retire that day.

Three years later, the man's wife called Robert's office and asked for a meeting. At that point, meeting with clients was no longer a typical part of Robert's day. However, when this client called, Robert was really looking forward to meeting the client. The meeting request was an unusual request coming from her, so Robert wondered what had happened.

On the day of the meeting, Robert walked into the conference room and was greeted by the woman and her sister. Robert was immediately concerned that Mike, the client's husband, wasn't with her. When the woman started crying—the tears were just streaming down her face—Robert said, "What happened?"

"Robert," the woman said, "Mike just passed away. If it wasn't for you, I wouldn't have spent the last three years with him. He would have been working. He was a workaholic. However, because you told him it was okay to retire, we were allowed to spend the last three years of his life together. I just wanted to say thank you."

This is the kind of impact you will have on clients if your mission extends beyond financial gains. As a result of truly caring about and helping your clients, you'll also have more success.

Those who fail to understand why they're working so hard will come to a dead stop when the going gets tough. They'll move onto something else and financial advisor will become a small date range on their LinkedIn profile. Pinpointing the motivation for your goals is the only thing that will get you through those tough moments. Anyone who has been in this industry for even a short period knows those moments are fast and furious.

Just like defining the *what* of your practice, defining the *why* is personal and it drives your mission. For some advisors, the mission is putting their kids through college or helping their kids buy their first home. One of my advisors wanted to provide a lifestyle so his wife could stay at home. Another wanted to donate $250,000 to his church by the end of the year.

Regardless of your *why*, define it, commit to it, and stick it on your goal board. Put it on a sticky note and slap it on your mirror. Put it in a place where you will see it every day so you're reminded, "This is what I'm doing and why I'm doing it." Get crazy with it! One of my advisors laminated his *why* and put it in the shower. No matter what he had to do each day, the first thing he saw was his *why*. It motivated him to keep going and work harder. Whether your *why* is with you in the shower, on a bedside table, or on a smartphone, keep it close. The moment you face rejection or an appointment falls through, that why needs to be at your fingertips. It's the only thing that will keep you going.

As soon as your *why* exists in the past, it can and should change. Focusing on the past is a road to nowhere.

Lose Your Why, Trade $400,000 for $40,000

One of my advisors was doing really well with her *why*—she wrote it down, verbally committed to it, and structured her day around it—and then it disappeared. After fifteen years of consistent success and $400,000 in annual revenue, she literally woke up and found her revenue had dropped to $40,000 a year.

I asked why she thought that happened.

She said, "Shawn, I lost my *why*."

Come to find out, she had been in a relationship with a person for some time and felt stable and comfortable. When the relationship fell apart, she didn't know what to do. What mattered before the relationship didn't seem to matter anymore. The picture she painted for her life totally changed. Her *why* had disappeared. Soon, hardship trickled into her business, and before she knew it, her business had crumbled.

A short time later, she changed her focus from what she lost to what she wanted for the future. She decided she wanted to pay for her grandkids' college tuition, take her daughters on an annual family trip, travel the world each year with her best friend, and experience new things. Her why was helping people. When she reflected on all of the people she was able to help in the past, she wanted that feeling again. As she changed focus, she once again found her *why*. Guess what? Her business got back on track! She had something to work toward.

It sounds so simple, but so few people actually take the time to define their *why*. Those who do, reach a much higher level of success than those who do not.

Here's another example. One of my top advisors, who was in his fifties and had been in the business for more than twenty-five years, was at a business conference having lunch with a group of peers who were about his age when someone raised the topic of living in the past.

The conversation went like this:

"Remember when we were first in the business? Those were the good old days. We had higher revenue products, sales were easier, and the marketing worked much better."

My advisor listened. Then he got up and walked to a table of younger advisors. Their conversation went like this:

"There's never been a better time to do what we do. There's so much opportunity, it's incredible."

The younger advisors were excited and thrilled to be in the business, while the older advisors were living in the past and grumbling about the good old days.

As a group, the sales numbers from the younger advisors were significantly higher than those of the older guys. But that wasn't the worst of it. The worst part was that if the older guys had put in the same effort as the younger advisors and used their experience to get more out of their activities, the younger advisors wouldn't have had a leg to stand on.

As fun as reminiscing may seem, dwelling on previous achievements is depressing and less fulfilling than focusing on present goals.

The same advisor who moved between the young advisors and the hardened warriors had a second story to share. One day, he woke up and found himself in a miserable place. He was grumpy, arrogant, discontent, and his business was the least productive it had been in twenty-five years. Adding insult to injury, he absolutely hated his job and going into the office.

Eventually he thought, "This business was so much fun. What changed?"

He realized his attitude had changed. Instead of looking forward, he kept looking at the past.

This advisor wasn't growing, and growth is where the fun is. From that day forward, he looked forward instead of back. He emptied his office of all trophies, plaques, and other reflections of past accomplishments, and decided to re-earn each by focusing on growth. Guess what happened? His business became fun again, and it started to grow.

There is so much wisdom in this story. The real joy—the real fun—is the pursuit of growth. It's doing more and being better instead of wanting due credit for past accomplishments. Few advisors realize this.

This business is full of ups and downs. Successful advisors stay the course, stay motivated, and focus on their personal missions. Small swings can interfere with productivity. You can't let them. Find what motivates you, and tap into it when a rough patch threatens. When you want to give up, return to your why, push through the low points, and know you're committed to reaching your goals. Mentally, you may experience turmoil, but business productivity must be constant.

Success is a self-fulfilling prophecy. If you don't have clear motivations for doing what you do, you will fail. You will fall victim to excuses. Instead of making one more appointment, you will leave the office early defeated, and with a mindset that today just isn't your day. Your mission will always supersede excuses. It will always keep you from giving up. It will always keep you looking forward instead of back.

GO ELITE

B O A R D

Chapter 2: Separate the Mission
from the Commission

Pinpointing the motivation for your goals is the only thing that will get you through those tough moments. Ask yourself:

1) Why am I in this business?

2) Why do I want to grow?

3) What is the real intent of my business?

3

GET IMPATIENT

"I find that the harder I work, the
more luck I seem to have."

—*Thomas Jefferson*

You know *what* you want and *why* you want it. Now it's
time to get it. You deserve it!

As you read this, roughly 300,000 other people are
trying to be financial advisors. Many will leave the game within
a year because they haven't developed the mental toughness critical to succeed in this industry. They're afraid of getting a no, they
run from challenges, and they latch onto excuses. By the time they
move on an idea, it's ancient history.

One common trait among top producers is impatience. When
they decide what they want, they hurry to get it. They recognize the
excuse, "there's always tomorrow," as the eighth deadly sin. Instead,
they make opportunity happen today. When it comes to our fears,
Lucius Annaeus Seneca says it best: "You act like mortals in all
that you fear, and like immortals in all that you desire." Just look at
Twitter. One day, Twitter's three founders said, "Hey, why don't we
find a new way to text each other?" They got to work immediately.
Two years later, Twitter was worth $1 billion. Pair great ideas with
impatience, put them to action, and incredible successes will happen
in a very short period of time.

Number of Years From Founding to $1 Billion Valuation

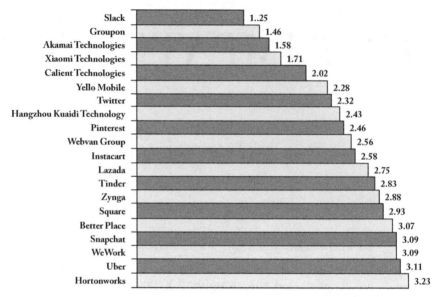

BI Intelligence

Source: PitchBook

The whole idea that it takes years to succeed is a myth. You can be a huge success in no time if you go after what you want with a sense of urgency. Successful advisors have an internal sense of urgency that constantly drives them toward doing, achieving, and moving. When it comes to success, they are extraordinarily impatient. They know a slow first step is a guarantee of last place. When they want to move, they do it quickly.

Avoid the Paralysis by Analysis Dilemma

Long before I started fastidiously taking notes on the country's top financial advisors, a little-known man named Elisha Gray developed a harmonic telegraph device. Its vibrating reeds transmitted musical tones—a pretty nifty concept in the summer of 1874. I don't know what else Gray was up to that summer. Maybe he joined the family on a few country escapes; maybe he visited with friends. Maybe he sat around his table thinking he had all the time in the world to perfect his little device before presenting it to the patent office. All I know is that Gray waited until December 1874 to test the device before his church and the public. He didn't diagram the device in his notebook until February 1875. When Gray brought that notebook to the United States patent office on February 14, 1879, he was three hours short of becoming one of the most recognized inventors in history. Alexander Graham Bell had filed a similar patent just three hours before.

While several legal proceedings followed and historians still enjoy a good back and forth regarding the true father of the telephone, the public by and large credits Bell with the invention. As you can imagine, this missed opportunity haunted Gray, whose feelings about the missed opportunity were found post-mortem.

> "The history of the telephone will never be fully written . . . It is partly hidden away . . . and partly lying on the hearts and consciences of a few whose lips are sealed—some in death and others by a golden clasp whose grip is even tighter."

Elite advisors move quickly to not miss opportunities like this. They avoid the paralysis by analysis dilemma, which happens when people spend so much time analyzing their next move, they never get around to moving. This applies to making appointments, setting and achieving goals, and developing marketing strategies. It applies to day-to-day activities and long-terms goals. No matter how small the idea, top advisors put ideas to action immediately.

A few years ago, I attended a conference. At the end, the speaker asked anyone who wanted to learn more to meet at the back of the room. It's no coincidence that our top-tier producers hurried to the back while our lower-tier producers watched and wondered what the hurry was. There's always tomorrow, right?

Seventy-Two Hours to Rapid Growth

It's somewhat ironic that advisors who have been in the game for four years sometimes out produce those who have been at it for twenty-five years. It's not that the more experienced advisors are no longer capable of leading the charge. It's not that they don't have great ideas. It's that they lose their impatience for putting ideas to action. When a great idea is shared, lower-tier producers ask, "What if this doesn't work?" Top advisors ask, "What if it does?" They act immediately with the confidence that the idea can and will work. Top advisors have an impatient urgency to put great ideas into practice immediately.

> Top advisors have an impatient
> urgency to put great ideas
> into practice immediately.

Moving fast doesn't mean getting sloppy or sacrificing quality. It means taking the first step immediately. If you discover a new idea for growing or improving your business, and you fail to implement it within seventy-two hours, you'll probably never do it. It will sit on the backburner, other things will get in the way, it will be forgotten, and it will lose its to-do list priority status. If you want to make a change, you've got seventy-two hours to do it.

To effectively use what I call the Seventy-Two-Hour Rule, assess your ideas, analyze them, and trust your instincts. I suggest listing your ideas, going through that list multiple times, and then ranking the five ideas you want to start within seventy-two hours.

To implement within 72 hours:

O Schedule a new seminar

O Update office

O Delegate a new task

While you may feel attached to each idea, cross off any that miss the top-five list. Focus your attention on the best ideas. The rest are often a waste of time. Trust your willingness to work through challenges and roadblocks while putting your ideas into action. Don't be afraid to adjust as you go. Momentum is on your side.

At a conference, one of our top advisors shared an idea that he implemented from a past training. The advisor next to me said the same idea was on his list, but he never got around to implementing it. You can imagine the difference in their productivity.

BOARD

Chapter 3: Get Impatient

Practice impatience:

1) List five ideas you feel would improve your current business

2) Rank them according to importance

3) Take the first step to implement the best idea within seventy-two hours

4

BECOME A STUDENT OF THE GAME

"If I have seen further than others, it is by standing upon the shoulders of giants."

—*Isaac Newton*

My first business aha moment occurred not long after I graduated from Kansas State University (KSU). I was a few months into my career and realized I didn't even know what I didn't know.

One day during a training, I explained this overwhelming *need to know* to a trainer. He said, "Why are you trying to figure everything out on your own?"

Why wasn't I asking questions of people who had worked in the business for twenty or thirty years? Why was I fumbling along trying to glean my own best practices when I had access to the industry's best and brightest? Think about it. I was surrounded by advisors who had spent a lifetime learning the right way to do things, why wouldn't I jump on the fast track and learn from them?

It was a great question that drove me to the bookstore where I bought five books related to the skillset my job required. Within a month, the books were smeared with highlights and filled with notes. I found answers to the questions I had been asking as well as answers to questions I hadn't even thought of yet.

I was immediately the most experienced person in my peer group: I had thirty to forty years of experience borrowed from experts. The result? I was the number-one salesperson in the office within three months. The concept of banking on the experiences of those who had been in my shoes for years gave me the know-how and confidence to excel.

As Ralph Waldo Emerson once said, "Every man I meet is my superior in some way. In that, I learn from him."

Your pursuit of the ideal practice must be relentless. Go to the bookstore, highlight the passages, absorb the text, ask the questions, and consult the experts. Do not reinvent the wheel. Become a student of the game. Learn from those who have gone before you, avoid their pitfalls, learn from their mistakes, and adopt their best practices. If you don't know an answer, ask a question. If the person you ask doesn't know, keep asking others. Do your research, read a book, or ask an expert.

An Open Mind Has Room for Knowledge

Barbara Sher, a best-selling author and lifestyle coach, says, "You can learn new things at any time in your life if you're willing to be a beginner. If you actually learn to like being a beginner, the whole world opens up to you."

She's saying, become a student of the game. You can absolutely learn something from everyone you talk to. Of all the pieces of advice I get from my advisors, "Learn something from everyone you know," is the one that lands in the echo chamber. They all say it. Many of them have mentors while others hire coaches. However you do it, make sure you're getting in front of people who you can learn from.

Henry, one of Advisor Excel's top advisors, grosses more than $1 million a year. When he joined Advisors Excel, we had dinner. I expected him to have a big ego and was hoping he was open-minded enough to hear some new ideas. Within ten minutes, he blew me away. The meeting was unlike any I'd had before. Henry was transparent about his issues and problems, open to making changes to his business, and wanted our advice about how he could improve by learning from other advisors. His openness made me momentarily forget he was a veteran—not a rookie. Why? Because even though it shouldn't be, his desire for constructive feedback tends to be uncommon in this business.

Fast-forward five years. Henry followed the advice and made more changes to his business than any advisor I've seen before or since and quadrupled his business. He was willing to ask questions, take advice, and learn from others. He was successful because he was, and still is, a student of the game.

Often times, an advisor will say, "I can't learn from someone who produces less than me."

Yet another producer will say, "I can learn something from everybody" and learn something from an advisor who produces a quarter of his business.

Regardless of production, you can learn something from everyone. One advisor may have a marketing funnel you don't currently have, but could add. Another might run a better business, or have better sales or management skills. Either way, you can and should learn something from everybody. Don't limit the knowledge you can gain to people who have a better number than you. Learn from everyone. As soon as you start looking for people to learn from, you'll find them. This is key.

Learn Something from Everyone

Remember my advisor who threw away all of his trophies so he could re-earn them? One of his best comments about that experience is, "Once you think you know something, you are dead."

I watched this willingness to learn play out among two very similar advisors. They had a lot in common. They were best friends, they lived within thirty miles of each other, went to the same college, studied the same subject, got similar grades, went into the business at the same time, and set similar production goals. Four years ago, they each did about $5 million in new assets a year. Today, one of them continues at $5 million. The other is consistently bringing in $20 million.

The advisor earning $20 million isn't more intelligent than the other. He doesn't communicate better, or have a better reputation. In fact, the only difference between him and his friend, who is producing $5 million, is that the $20 million earner became a student of the game. He studies the industry, learns from advisors, and takes advantage of industry seminars. He even listens to audiobooks while driving. His friend, on the other hand, listens to music. There's nothing wrong with music, but if you want to master your craft and become a student of the game, take every opportunity available to learn more. Not only did the $20 million earner learn a lot, he applied that knowledge to his own practice. The advisor who wasn't growing didn't invest any time or money in filling his head with knowledge.

So which advisor are you? The exception to the rule, or the one who's just like everyone else? Let's find out. I once heard that 90 percent of books don't get read past the first chapter, meaning most people read one chapter and leave the book on the shelf to collect dust. I bet the 10 percent who do finish represent the same minority who reach incredible levels of success. They exist outside the norm because they are disciplined to go the extra mile. So, are you committed to finish *Breakthrough*? Or, are you going with the majority and closing the book or turning off the Kindle after these first few chapters? The choice is yours.

Regardless of how you learn, become a student of the game. Be aware of what's going on around you. Adapt, ask questions, and grow. Go to industry training seminars, hear how others have hit new levels of success, and continually improve by surrounding yourself with people who expand your belief in what's possible.

Surround Yourself with the Best

One of my top advisors went from $10 million a year in new assets in 2008, to more than $100 million in new assets in 2014. At a conference, I asked him, "What is the single biggest factor in your success in this business?"

He thought for a minute, rattled off two quick ideas, and went back to the conference.

Three hours later, he came back and said, "Shawn, I've thought about your question. I think the biggest factor in my success is that when I go to events like this, I'm constantly surrounded by advisors who do twice as much as me, or who have a better business model than mine. Seeing someone else double my production has played a huge role. It helps me expand my limits and self-limiting beliefs. I tell myself, 'You know what? If he or she can do that, I can do it, too.' These are normal people, not super humans, and if they can do it, I can do it. Over time, I learn what they're doing, how they're doing it and why they're doing it, and it has rubbed off on me and made me better."

That gray matter between your ears is one of the main reasons you're either a top producer or struggling to pay bills. It holds self-limiting beliefs such as "that's not possible." Surrounding yourself with people who say "everything is possible" reverses that mentality.

Take a look at this historic example. On December 17, 1903, the Wright Brothers made history when they successfully completed the first human-controlled flight. In that instant, they shattered the mental barrier humans held for thousands of years that human flight was impossible. On July 20, 1969, just sixty-six years later, the Apollo 11 spacecraft landed on the moon, shattering beliefs that space travel was impossible for humans. The most important thing the Wright Brothers taught us wasn't how to fly. It was that flight is possible for humans. We see this pattern in other areas of human achievement as well.

Nobody on earth had run a mile in less than four minutes until Roger Bannister did it on May 6, 1954. When he broke that barrier, a switch flipped and runners around the world thought, "If he can run a four-minute mile, why can't I?"

The previous world record of 4:01 lasted nine long years, but Bannister's record of 3:59 lasted forty-six days. His rival, John Landy, destroyed it. During the next three years, sixteen more runners ran the mile in less than four minutes. The point is, like successful runners who study elite runners, successful advisors constantly study other elite advisors because studying them proves that the impossible is possible. So ask yourself, "Do I surround myself with elite advisors who are willing to share best practices with me?"

Some of life's biggest decisions and accomplishments are influenced by those around us, a concept that's been validated by Harvard professor Dr. David McClelland. McClelland conducted a twenty-five year study that concluded the single most influential factor for success is a person's reference group.

Are You Getting in Your Own Way?

If you don't think it's possible to be a seven-, eight-, or nine-figure producer, you never will be. Self-limiting behavior will always hold you back. Hang out with people who are doing better than you are. Each new record that's set expands our belief in what's possible. What one person can do, any one person can do. Seeing others accomplish something provides a sense of certainty that we can do it as well.

> What one person can do, any one person can do. Seeing others accomplish something provides a sense of certainty that we can do it as well.

As the legendary personal development speaker Jim Rohn once said, we are the average of the five people we spend the most time with. If your five people are less motivated and earn less than you do, you'll eventually fall to their level. If those five are highly motivated and earn significantly more than you do, they'll bring you to their level.

So pick your peers and partners wisely. Find the right five people to surround yourself with. Once you find them, ask them exactly how they did what they've done. What you'll learn might shock you. Sometimes, simple things make all the difference in the world.

Don't limit your five people to people who make more money than you. Choose those who market better, run their businesses more efficiently, or have a better office structure. Commit to learn, study, and implement the secrets of their success. Ask them about key changes to their business that have broken perceived ceilings and achieved new heights. Express genuine gratitude for what you learn and share your own successes and ideas in return. Do this, and you'll go further than you ever thought possible. You'll also reach milestones faster than those who have gone before you.

If you're not currently hanging out with people who think big, start attending industry trainings and events. Take three days and travel to an industry event, get a business coach, or get to know people outside your industry who excel in ways that can benefit you.

One of the keys to Advisors Excel's success is that our entire culture was developed around the idea of giving outstanding advisors the opportunity to share ideas. Every year, our advisors have six to ten opportunities to spend time together, share best practices, and learn from each other. They learn together, they share what's working, and the whole group improves because of it.

Ask for Criticism

Iron sharpens iron. The more you learn, the sharper you'll become, and the more you'll achieve. This means constantly learning *and* being open to criticism.

A few years ago, one of my top advisors got off stage after delivering a killer presentation that made the crowd go absolutely crazy. He walked over to me at break and said, "What could I have done better?"

He was asking for criticism, which put me in a tough spot because he'd done so well. What a strange thing to ask, right? After a good—or mediocre —presentation,most people want a pat on the back, reassurance that they did a good job. Not this guy. He wanted honest, critical feedback on his entire performance from his delivery to his engagement and his content. So whatever you do in your business—whether it's an event, radio show, or appointment process—ask for feedback from others. Have someone you respect and trust review your process and give you candid feedback. This sounds so simple, yet people rarely do it.

One of the many things I've learned working with top advisors is that they're never satisfied. For them, success has no end point, no finish line. They ask for critiques and opinions from those they trust. They genuinely want to improve, and they take those criticisms in stride. They accept them, ask questions, and use the advice to sharpen their axe and improve their business. These advisors welcome the opportunity to punch holes in their way of doing things.

> One of the many things I've learned working with top advisors is that they're never satisfied. For them, success has no end point, no finish line.

Obsession—It's Not a Bad Thing

While people don't always associate the word obsession with positive outcomes, obsession in the right hands can be a good thing. Obsession is nothing more than having a certain topic occupy your mind consistently.

NBA player Kobe Bryant said that when he first joined the NBA, he was surprised to learn that other players didn't take the game as seriously as he did. While they practiced and did what they had to do to get by, Bryant let basketball and the skills he needed to succeed consume his every thought. Guess what happened? Bryant became one of the greatest players in the league.

Advisors who are obsessed with their practices never leave their success to chance. They calculate their every move to make sure they're giving themselves the highest probability for success. Mediocre advisors just look for excuses to not get things done.

I guarantee the success story you're looking for is out there. Be at the top of your game at all times, be willing to change, constantly seek improvement, and surround yourself with great people.

GO ELITE
B O A R D

Chapter 4: Become a Student of the Game

Learn something from everyone you know.

1) List three things you want to know about or improve in your business

2) List the resources—people, books, websites, blogs—that can lead you to those answers

3) Send an email or call the resources on those lists and start answering those questions

5

TAKE CONSISTENT, CONSTANT ACTION

"The way to get started is to quit
talking and start doing."

— *Walt Disney*

You can talk all day about goals, desires, and missions, but it's what you do that counts.

As NBA player Kevin Durant said, "Hard work beats talent when talent fails to work hard."

Commit to the Right Activity, Get the Right Results

Nothing replaces hard work. If you're committed to building your best practice, commit to generating an insane amount of the *right* activity.

The majority of successful advisors I work with got started in this business using failure-prone models such as cold calling, door knocking, and cold lead chasing. They begged for "yeses" but always got "nos."

I've been behind the desk, punching 130 sets of phone numbers into a phone in a single day, praying the person on the other end would be nice or—at the very least—not rude. I've stood there shaking, wondering if I was setting myself up for a stranger to ruin my day. The first week of cold calling is rough. None of us like it at first. In fact, many of my top advisors hated cold calling. However, week two is more comfortable than week one. During week three, the fear all but disappears. Week four sees the fear go completely and it's just another day.

You have to wonder, did the type of exposure so many of us complain about guide their success? No matter how tough it is to grasp sometimes, constant rejection and learning to bounce back from it made them better advisors. For top advisors, cold calling led to strong work habits and an early exposure to rejection. After failing over and over again, they weren't afraid of "no." Early on, they were okay with failure, understood the value of a lead, and developed thick skin. They clearly got the idea that every "no" is closer to a "yes."

> Your success over the long haul
> directly correlates with how
> hard you're willing to work.

A person who earns his or her fortune independently tends to do better than someone who is handed an inheritance. People who learn the hard way are more responsible and soar to a higher level than those who have it easy. Think about a spoiled kid who never works for anything. Will that kid do better than the neighbor kid who worked full-time all summer bailing hay in the sun? It's doubtful. This applies to advisors. The one who cuts his or her teeth day in and day out develops the necessary skills and the mentality for long-term success.

Often, I'll talk with an advisor who will look at another advisor and say, "I want that." The problem is, the business they want is *today's* business. They don't see what it took for the other advisor to reach today. They don't see the experiences that shaped the advisor's career. They don't see the sleepless nights, sacrifices, and late evenings. They don't see the relentless amount of effort that advisor expended to build his or her business.

When one of my top advisors started, he maxed out his credit cards to fund his marketing efforts. He was basically broke and had no backup plan. Finally, he got a break. He wrote a case that generated a $15,000 commission[1]. Unfortunately, a week later, the woman changed her mind on the life insurance case. He felt he'd reached the end of the world and wasn't sure how he'd continue, but he kept pushing. Today, he's one of the most successful advisors I know.

You may see an incredibly successful advisor who works four days a week *today*, but remember, life wasn't always that way. To achieve today's success, that advisor worked six days a week for years. You can't jump to today. You've got to work hard and put in the time. Your success over the long haul directly correlates with how hard you're willing to work.

Here's a tangible example as to how hard work can benefit you. So let's say you were one of those advisors who grew up in the business smiling and dialing. You were handed a list of people to cold call, and your job was to convince them to meet with you in person.

Let's say we have an office where most advisors call an average of seventy people a day. About 20 percent—or fourteen of those—result in a call with a live prospect. Those prospects can

---

1 In this book, we often use examples where we include commission numbers or revenue earned. Please note that every example includes arbitrary numbers that were handpicked for clarity and simplicity. They are not meant to justify any amount of revenue or commission.

then be broken into thirds:

- The first third will pass, no matter what you say or what approach you take
- The second third will say yes no matter what
- The third is up for grabs. They're open-minded, but their decision to lean yes or no depends entirely on you

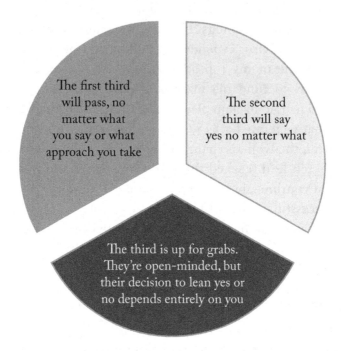

So if everybody calls seventy people a day and you call 140 people, you speak with twenty-eight prospects instead of fourteen. Based on the thirds breakout, regardless of what you do, you have nine fairly easy sales. In addition to creating more opportunity for yourself by working hard, you gain more experience and improve, which will lead to more sales. The average person calling seventy people has four easy sales. If they are a much better sales person and convert every up for grabs prospect, they still only get the same result as you. We'll talk in more detail about how to strengthen your position within these groups of thirds later on.

Your success in this business directly correlates to how many people you see. If you see twice as many people as someone else, even if they are a better sales person, they will have an uphill battle to beat your numbers. You can be the best financial planner or money manager in the world, but if you don't have people to see, you won't be successful.

Your success in this business directly correlates to how many people you see.

How to Crush Sales Goals Every Time

Most advisors meet one-to-two new people a week. My top advisor meets four new people *a day*. A day. That's an insane amount of activity. As you can imagine, everyone always asks how he does it. The thing is, he's much younger than most advisors and has only been in the business for a few years, yet he beats advisors with more than twenty years of experience. Why? Because he works harder than everyone else and focuses on seeing people.

At an event, my advisor, Bill, was sort of bragging about how he received more than forty referrals the previous year. One of my top advisors, Craig, overheard Bill and said, "How many?"

With pride, Bill said, "Forty."

Straight faced, Craig looked at Bill and said, "That is not nearly enough."

At first Bill was a little offended however, his opinion changed a couple of hours later when Craig walked across the stage. We'd just welcomed him by announcing he was one of Advisors Excel's top producers. Later, Bill told me he learned a huge lesson that day—he was thinking too small and needed to find a way to see more people.

Most advisors set goals by looking at new assets instead of looking at what they have to do every day to reach that goal. So not only are they working hard, they're working *smart*. They're focused on exactly what they need to do to reach their goals.

Say your production goal is $20 million in new assets. Do you know what must be done every day, week, and month to achieve that goal? If your answer is, "I'll reach the $20 million mark by seeing more people," you're being too vague. You're also not thinking like an elite advisor. Don't worry, you're not alone. When it comes to setting goals, elite advisors never move through the year on a hope and a prayer. Instead, they reverse-engineer their plan. They know *exactly* what must be done each week to crush that goal by the end of the year.

To understand what must be done every day to reach $20 million in new assets, find your average case size, which is total assets divided by the average number of sales made. For this example[2], let's say case size is $250,000.

Next, look at your closing ratio. Closing ratio is determined by how many first or new appointments are made in a year. To calculate yours, look at your previous year's appointment calendar and identify all first appointments. Only count the ones that completed the sales cycle. If for every five appointments one new client was closed, that's a 20 percent (1:5) sales ratio.

To reach $20 million in new assets for the year, you have to know how many people you need to see. To do that, we divide the goal by average case size. For this example, it's $20,000,000 / $250,000 for a total of eighty. Eighty new clients must be brought on to reach $20 million. Dividing eighty new clients by a closing ratio of 20 percent shows 400 new appointments must be made to close eighty people. Working a forty-week year, this requires ten appointments a week.

---

2 For the purpose of this exercise and others throughout the book, I will use numbers that are sufficient for the example. For each equation, you will need to apply your own numbers to the model to produce accurate results for your situation,

Goal $20,000,000
÷ Average Case Size $250,000

= 80 Clients

80 New Clients
÷ 20% Closing Ratio

= 400 New Appointments

Get Specific and Get It Done

To hit $20 million, you have to know exactly what you need to do each week to get there. For the above example, you'd need to see ten people a week. It does not get much clearer than that.

GOALS

Increase marketing by 10%

Reduce staff turnover

Launch new website

~~$20,000,000 in production~~
Appts 10x a week

It's much easier to know what you
have to do each week to achieve a
big annual goal than it is to stick a
giant number above your computer
and hope for the best. If you
want to become an elite advisor,
get specific and then get busy.

It's much easier to know what you have to do each week to achieve a big annual goal than it is to stick a giant number above your computer and hope for the best. If you want to become an elite advisor, get specific and then get busy.

QUICK GOAL SETTING TIP:

Production isn't the ultimate goal, profitability is. Don't focus on premium alone. If annuity premiums increased by $2 million last year, but cost $150,000 in additional marketing to get there, it's a backpedal. Focusing on premium alone doesn't show the whole picture.

If you commit to scheduling ten appointments a week, or meeting eight new people a week, do it. Activity directly relates to behavior, and yours must match what you say. If you say you want to grow, don't spend twenty-five to thirty hours in the office. Don't say you're too busy to take more appointments if you leave work early on Fridays.

Find the Value in Every No

Write out your specific, day-to-day goals, make connecting with more people a top priority, and put those goals in motion within the next seventy-two hours. Now, I'm not recommending you start cold calling prospects, but I will say getting rejected time and time again has a way of helping advisors later on. In this business, skin thickens as you learn every "no" is that much closer to a "yes." The more you try, the more you're rejected, the more accustomed you become to both "nos" and "yeses." My top advisors are almost bulletproof to rejection. They've made enough calls, hosted enough events, and heard enough "nos" that "no" doesn't affect them emotionally. When they hear it, they just move on. No problem. The work ethic developed during this period stays with these advisors as they evolve and find better ways to market and run their business.

No one can walk into this business expecting to work 10 a.m. to 3 p.m. every day with eight weeks off a year and expect phenomenal success. You've got to work hard and see people. If you're bringing in $6 million a year in new assets, seeing five people a week, and want to double your business, see ten new people a week. Bring in as much activity as possible, and watch your business expand.

B O A R D

Chapter 5: Take Consistent, Constant Action

Are you setting yourself up for success? Ask yourself the following:

1) Am I putting in enough hours today to build the business I hope to have in the future?

2) Do I know specifically how many people I need to see every day to reach my current goal?

3) Am I seeing enough people every week to reach this goal?

SECTION 1:
MASTER THE GAME
SUMMARY

It's impossible to know where you're going without some kind of map. Take a few minutes and define what you want from your business and why you want it. Remember that a why driven by financial incentives alone will not sustain you through the rough patches.

Elite advisors are driven by a strong desire to help people. Once you decide on the intention behind your business, do what elite advisors do: roll up your sleeves, and get to work. Get familiar with your numbers, and figure out exactly how many people you need to see today to reach your goals. Write your goals somewhere you can see them, and develop strong work habits. Don't set a goal of $10 million in new assets and then work twelve hours a week. Make every one of your daily activities count toward your goals.

When you have an idea, roll it out within seventy-two hours. Get impatient and don't be afraid to ask for help. None of us know everything, but that doesn't stop elite advisors from constantly learning. Read, listen to, and connect with people who are where you want to be. Master your game.

SUMMARY

Section 1: Master the Game

**Top Three GO Elite Actions
to Master Your Game**

1) Define the *what* and *why* of your business, and put both in a place where you can see them *every single day*

2) Crunch the numbers to specifically outline what you need to do every day to reach your goals and develop work habits that will move you toward that goal

3) Connect with five people who know something you don't who can help your business

MASTER MARKETING

"Our job is to connect people, to interact with them in a way that leaves them better than we found them, more able to get where they'd like to go."

— *Seth Godin*

You know what you want, why you want it, and what attitude you must have to get it. Time for some nuts and bolts. The truth is, sometimes we make this business a lot more complex than it really is. Simply put, this business is actually three businesses in one: marketing, sales, and operations.

Marketing attracts prospects, sales converts them to clients, and operations supports your business, your team, and your clients. You can't be good at marketing, but ignore sales or operations, or love sales, and ignore marketing. The key is to develop a business that fires on all three cylinders. Think of this business as a stool. If one leg is rickety, the whole thing will go over.

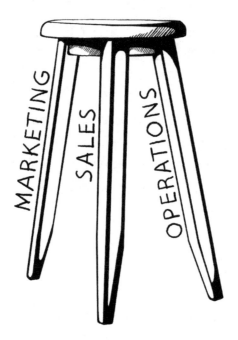

Once, I asked a top producer who had experienced some struggles in his business, "What moment turned your career around? When did you figure it out?"

He said, "When I realized this business isn't about stocks, mutual funds, bonds, or any other financial tool. It's when I realized this business is a marketing business."

However you define it, marketing is the driving force behind growth in this business. Your marketing strategy determines how many people you see, how many appointments you set, and how many clients you get. Ignore marketing and forget about building a successful business. It won't happen.

Too many advisors don't realize the importance of marketing and instead spend time analyzing plans and doing case preparation. Others talk themselves out of marketing. They say it's too expensive or it doesn't work. They don't realize the key to success is marketing. In fact, the greatest expense in this business is having an open calendar with no one to see, which depends entirely on marketing.

I often look at advisors who are brilliant, educated people and assume they're hugely successful. When I find out they're struggling, I think, "Why aren't they a top producer?"

Every single time, the answer is this: They're terrible at marketing. On paper, they have everything. They're well-spoken and have a good image, yet instead of superstardom, they struggle. These advisors look at advisors who they think are less knowledgeable, experienced, polished, or articulate and wonder why they are doubling or tripling their production. They wonder, "How is she producing more than I am? I'm twice the advisor she is."

They assume the other advisor has an unfair advantage and they make excuses. Maybe the other advisor is in a better area, has less competition and higher net-worth clients, or comes from a well-connected family. Instead of fixing their own problems, these advisors turn themselves into victims. They think, "If people only knew how much more I do for my clients, if people only saw the difference between us, I would be the one with higher production numbers."

This line of thinking makes this business more complicated than it is and misses the point. It isn't knowledge or image alone that boosts production. It's marketing. Marketing is everything.

It isn't knowledge or image
alone that boosts production. It's
marketing. Marketing is everything.

Think about it. You can be the best financial advisor in the state, the country, or even the world, but no one will know about you unless you market well. Without marketing, you're the best-kept secret out there. Good for a secret sauce, terrible for a financial advisor.

If you fall into the group of advisors who know what marketing is but grumble every time someone like me goes on about the importance of marketing, consider this—what if the problem is the way you understand marketing? What if you are making it harder than it has to be?

Years ago, one of my advisors said he hated hosting seminars. When I asked for details, he went into his seminar process, which involved sending mailers, taking calls, showing up to events, setting up, talking to a room of thirty-five people, breaking down, and driving home. By the time he finished the seminar, he was worn out, irritated, and one hundred percent convinced seminars weren't for him.

After every seminar he said, "I've got to quit doing these."

He didn't care about the results. He was too focused on the process and how much he disliked it so he used every excuse in the book to avoid seminars. He would say, "I'm not doing a seminar next month because it's the summer," or, "I'm not doing a seminar in December because I've got a holiday party."

In terms of results, we knew the seminars were working, so we started finding ways to make the process better for him. We suggested that he train a key staff member to set up and breakdown each seminar. My advisor was dubious, gave it a try, and was pleasantly surprised. Delegating that one task to another person for minimal expense gave my advisor time to prepare for his seminars. Instead of going on stage irritated and drained, he got his head in the game, practiced exactly what he wanted to say, and worked through how to maximize audience engagement. On stage, he was energetic and interesting. The process he hated became someone else's to manage. Not surprisingly, the audience responded better and he scheduled more appointments.

By simplifying one element of this advisor's marketing strategy, we changed his attitude toward marketing altogether.

I had a similar advisor who was so afraid of losing control of his seminars that his staff would stand to the side while he set up. Even if he struggled to set up his PowerPoint, they waited because they knew he wanted to do everything himself.

Both advisors in these examples suffered from what I call The Advisor Curse. The Advisor Curse occurs when an advisor does too much out of fear that no one else will do the task as well as he or she will. The Advisor Curse is ineffective and creates a lot of headaches for advisors and staff. Letting staff help is critical to developing an effective business. We will talk more about how to do this and avoid the Advisor Curse in later chapters.

If you're one of those advisors who thinks you don't enjoy marketing, examine each of your marketing processes and identify what you don't like about them. These processes may be something you shouldn't be doing in the first place, such as setting up, or breaking down seminars. Make the process easier so you can focus on what you do best, which is sharing your message.

Once you tweak your process to make marketing more effective and enjoyable, examine your funnels. Hundreds of advisors legitimately have no idea if their marketing efforts are costing or contributing money to their business. If you don't know whether your marketing funnels are creating money for your business or costing your business money, you won't know if they're working.

Over time, these funnels will change, grow, and diversify. And, if you follow the advice outlined in these chapters, you'll understand how analyzing your marketing numbers, targeting your key audience, and setting appointments with higher-quality clients can grow your business.

OBJECTIVES

Section 2: Master Marketing

In this section, you will learn how to:

- View marketing as an investment rather than an expense
- Stop wasting money on branding
- Develop congruent, direct marketing strategies
- Analyze your marketing funnels
- Diversify marketing funnels based on actual data
- Turn today's "nos" into tomorrow's "yeses"
- Avoid lulls in your marketing efforts
- Assess the value of your appointments

6

MASTER YOUR CASH FLOW

"Don't be afraid to spend money on marketing."
— *Elite Advisor, MO*

O ver the years, I've had many advisors tell me that they aren't doing much marketing because it's just too expensive for them. True, marketing can be expensive, and some marketing efforts are more expensive than others, but I'd argue the biggest expense in your business is not having people to see.

Earn $4 for Every $1 Spent

If you put $1 in a slot machine, pulled the handle, and $4 came out, you'd pour money into the machine, right? Soon a significant amount of your "gambling" budget would go into that machine, right?

Now, think of that slot machine as your marketing budget. You put $1 in and get a return of $4. Would you feed your marketing budget as frequently and with as much enthusiasm as you did the slot machine?

The question to ask about marketing expenses isn't, "How much should I *spend* on marketing?" It's, "How much should I *invest* in marketing"?

I asked one of the top advisors at Advisors Excel who tripled his business within five years to pinpoint the number one factor in his growth. He said, "Don't be afraid to spend money on marketing."

Your Power Cash-Flow Equation

This business is front-loaded. Spending money on marketing generates calls, which results in revenue. The more you market, the more people come to see you, the more revenue earned. It's a simple equation:

$$\text{Outflow} = \text{Inflow} = \text{Cash Flow}$$

Think about it this way. How much does it cost not to market? Say you have ten appointments. You close three. Each of those new clients is worth $10,000 in revenue, so you make $30,000 every time you bring in ten appointments. Every week you miss out on those appointments, your team loses $30,000. That's the cost of *not* marketing. This brings me to a major point. Do you know your numbers? Do you know your closing ratio, what an appointment costs, or what each appointment is worth to your business?

Expense or Investment?

One time an advisor complained to me about the cost of her $50,000 radio budget. I then asked, "How many appointments did that get you?"

She had no idea. Ninety-nine percent of advisors have no idea what their numbers are. This advisor listed a $50,000 expense on her income statement without knowing how many appointments it got her or what the appointments were worth.

Ninety-nine percent of advisors have no idea what their numbers are.

Let's say radio got her fifty new prospects and she had a closing ratio of 5:1. If each client is worth $15,000 in revenue and she gets ten, that's $150,000. Looks like that marketing "expense" actually yielded $100,000 in net revenue. When you look at it that way, marketing isn't an expense. It's an investment.

> 10 New Clients $150,000
> - Marketing Cost $50,000
> _____
> **= $100,000 in Revenue**

Most advisors would see a phenomenal uptick in their marketing efforts if they viewed the cost/benefit of each marketing funnel—radio, TV, and seminars—the way the CEO of a *Fortune* 500 company would. If you're not tracking the outcomes of your marketing efforts, how do you know if they're working? How can an advisor possibly know if a $50,000 radio spend is expensive if she doesn't know how much revenue it generates?

Advisors have a natural tendency to want to get a better deal and find a cheaper solution. In this case, the advisor made a great return on a $50,000 investment … she just didn't know it.

Marketing vs. Branding

Not only do you need to know the cost/benefit of each marketing funnel, you also need to understand what marketing *is*. Branding is not marketing. It looks like marketing, it might even smell like marketing, but when you're a small business, spending on branding takes valuable resources away from your marketing budget.

Marketing brings new clients through the door. Branding determines how your clients *identify* your business. If you put marketing money into branding, but it doesn't bring people in, you need to revisit how you're spending your money. Understanding this is hugely important.

I had one advisor who paid for a billboard. He loved it because people recognized him at church and around town. His kids loved it, too, but what did it do for his business? Nothing. Once you learn how to market well, you'll get the branding for free. People will start recognizing and reacting to your brand. First you have to get them through the door by marketing to them.

A 10 Percent Solution to Higher Profit Margins

One of my advisors, Tony, marketed heavily and made $1 million in gross revenue, but had a net income of $250,000. Simple math shows his profit margin was 25 percent. When I told Tony he could have a profit margin of 35 percent, he was shocked. He said, "There's no way I could have a profit margin like that. I don't know how that's possible in this business."

We worked on Tony's profit margin and crunched the numbers. The 10 percent separation between Tony's 25 percent profit margin and the 35 percent profit margin other advisors had came down to Tony's marketing budget.

I looked at Tony's seminar numbers, which were fine, but then I hit a big expense labeled billboards. Tony had listed billboards as a marketing expense. I said, "Tony, the purpose of marketing is to get appointments."

Tony agreed.

I said, "So how many appointments have your billboards generated?"

Come to find out, Tony's $100,000 a year billboard expense didn't directly generate any appointments. Sure, the billboards made him feel good, but they didn't produce tangible results. They didn't directly impact the number of appointments Tony made. Interestingly, Tony's belief that the billboards were working came from word-of-mouth feedback only. A few seminar attendees saw the billboards, but that isn't the point. Billboards can help get your name out there, but a $100,000 expense should produce direct results, not just help influence other marketing efforts. The primary driver is getting clients to respond. In Tony's case, the billboards did not do this.

EXPENSES		REVENUE
Radio	-$50,000	$150,000
Public Events	-$75,000	$100,000
Billboards	-$100,000	$0*

*But it made me feel good

The 10 percent difference between Tony and other advisors was his billboard expense. Tony chose to have his name recognized by friends instead of choosing an additional $100,000 for his business.

Every good advisor spends money on branding instead of marketing at some point in their career. Good advisors learn to brand themselves while also getting a direct response. They may have a billboard, or a spot on a local financial radio show that's fun, but doesn't get the phones ringing. Both make them feel good, both get their name out there, but there's a huge difference between feeling good and generating revenue. Branding is great for *Fortune* 500 companies, businesses that have money to spend on marketing and branding, but for a small business, spending money on marketing should be the top priority.

Work to generate appointments, and you'll simultaneously build a brand for free. Why? Because when people see your name over and over again, they'll start recognizing your brand. This type of repetition affects the subconscious and keeps you at the forefront of your target market's mind.

Repetition affects the subconscious.
Repetition affects the subconscious.
Repetition affects the subconscious.
Repetition affects the subconscious.
Repetition affects the subconscious.
Repetition affects the subconscious.
Repetition affects the subconscious.
Repetition affects the subconscious.
Repetition affects the subconscious.
Repetition affects the subconscious.
Repetition affects the subconscious.

While marketing and branding can work together, it's important that as a small business owner, you invest in marketing, not branding.

Chapter 6: Master Your Cash Flow

To make a smart investment in your marketing strategy:

1) Calculate how many appointments each marketing funnel generates

2) Understand how much each appointment is worth and how much revenue each funnel generates

3) Don't put a large percentage of your marketing dollars into branding

7

SPEAK YOUR CLIENTS' LANGUAGE

"Marketing is a contest for people's attention."
— *Seth Godin*

The goal of every marketing effort is to see more people. The more access points you have for contacting people, the more people you'll talk to. This is where direct response marketing and congruent marketing come in.

Direct response marketing, which is anything that allows you to send your marketing message and get an immediate response, may include direct mail, seminars, radio ads, radio shows, TV ads, TV shows, and the Internet and is designed to get people to take action now. It's a big fishing net and it moves in an ascending cost order from direct mail to the Internet. Instead of talking to ten people a day, a mailer grabs 10,000, and a radio or TV show grabs hundreds of thousands. A bigger net hits a larger audience, but it also costs more. However, keep in mind that sometimes a bigger expense yields better results.

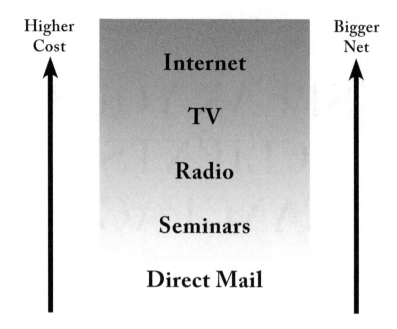

Higher Cost

Bigger Net

Internet

TV

Radio

Seminars

Direct Mail

It takes time to build marketing efforts and cast a wide net. Starting out, your net will be fairly small. Maybe you mail 10,000 people to come to a seminar. Say that you host two nights and forty people come each night. In total, you see eighty people once a month. As you grow and add seminars, you'll see eighty people a few times a month, netting 240 people per month. Let's say in a few years, you invest in a radio spot. Your net grows to 100,000 listeners. If you're consistent with your marketing efforts, stick with what works, slowly add new marketing funnels, and track your successes. Your net will continue to grow as you become more successful. The bigger your net, the bigger your potential results.

Another important factor in marketing is making sure your marketing is congruent with your message. Congruent marketing ensures that your marketing tactics align with your firm's core message.

Cut through the Noise

Think about it this way. Say you're driving with your spouse. You hear something really interesting on the radio. When you tell them about it, they have no idea what you're talking about. They look at you as if you're crazy and you're sitting there wondering how they could have missed something so awesome. Were they even in the car?

When a person technically hears what's going on around them, but only absorbs the pieces relevant to them, it's called selective intake. Selective intake is an issue marketers battle daily. Say you send a mailer. A potential client opens it at breakfast while drinking coffee and helping one kid get dressed while he helps the other make a sandwich and also flips through email. Not only is your message competing with each of these distractions, it has very little chance of being received. Your message has to be so compelling that it speaks right to your audience so you can interrupt their pattern.

When you develop marketing strategies and materials, you must be 100 percent in tune with your audience and the messages you want to communicate to that audience. The more thought you put into the mailer that's competing with breakfast, email, and kids, the more likely you are to get their attention.

Congruent marketing forces us to *specifically* advertise what we're best at so we can attract appropriate clients who we are best able to help. Congruent marketing aligns your end point—what you're attracting people to—with what you're offering. It places you, your client, and your staff on the same page.

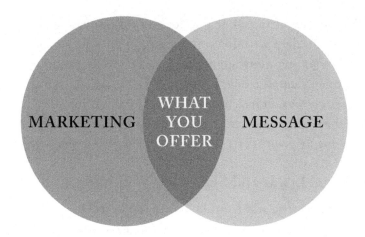

For example, if you're best equipped to help people who have $500,000 or more in investable assets, your message must convey that. What you say on the radio and what you offer on a direct mail piece must coincide with the message given to clients when they visit the office, and your team must provide the relevant skills to $500,000 clients when they come through the door.

Many advisors latch onto any message they can think of to attract clients. If the hot topic in the area is Medicare or Medicaid, they tailor their marketing materials and seminars toward Medicare or Medicaid. If their ideal goal is to talk about investments or life insurance, talking about Medicare or Medicaid is not congruent. That's called baiting and switching. This makes the sales process much more difficult while also frustrating the consumer. It also doesn't get the right prospects in front of advisors and is arguably unethical.

One of my advisors used to run joint seminars with an attorney. The attorney advertised estate planning, and my advisor and the attorney split presentation time. My advisor saw an opportunity to market and went for it even though the marketing had nothing to do with his core messages or skills. Naturally, every attendee wanted to talk about trusts and wills. Great for the attorney. Terrible for the advisor. My advisor's staff spent their time trying to convince the audience to meet with my advisor about a topic they weren't initially interested in.

My advisor attracted people for the wrong reasons. His marketing didn't align with his core messages, or what he could offer. Instead of getting more appointments, my advisor generated fewer appointments and the ones he did generate had a much lower closing ratio. He should have brought people in based on his strengths rather than bringing them in based on a topic they cared about that he couldn't help with. His results would have been much better.

Get More Leads and Skyrocket Your Closing Rate

Only advertise what you know you do best. Do not market to fill seats with just anyone. Market to fill seats with the *right* people. Practice congruency. Identify your goals and strengths. Then, develop messages that *promote* those over and over and over again.

Do not market to fill seats
with anyone. Market to fill
seats with the *right* people.

There are hundreds of tricky ways to backdoor people into the office, but that's the wrong approach to marketing and building a long-term, sustainable business. Bring people in for the right reasons. Be direct about what you want to accomplish, and attract the people who need the type of help you can offer.

One of our top advisors hosted a seminar that was all about annuities. He was a great annuities professional, and felt annuities would benefit others. His seminar was all about annuities, from the beginning to the end. Guess who he attracted? People interested in annuities. His seminar was straight to the point and, as a result, was a huge success.

Another advisor focused on income planning. Income planning in the mailer, income planning at the seminar, income planning during his meetings. Income planning—that's all he does. People don't talk to him about stocks, Medicaid, or bonds. They literally come in specifically for income planning.

The people walking through your door must be the right ones. Contrary to what we've been taught, it's better to have five good prospects at your door than fifty who aren't a good fit.

If you're looking for clients with more than $250,000 to invest, your marketing messages need to speak to that audience. The same goes for $100,000 clients or $1 million clients. You cannot tailor a message to the $250,000 investor and expect to get calls from someone looking to invest $1 million.

Think of your marketing message like those Google or Facebook ads that pop up on your computer or smartphone. The ads always relate to your most recent search. If you looked up hiking gear, poker tables, or books on business, I guarantee ads related to each will follow. The many minds behind this kind of targeted advertising know their market. They know that if you've been looking at backcountry backpacks, you might click on a glossy ad for hiking boots. Your marketing strategy must do the same.

Attract Your Ideal Clients

An advisor I know targeted potential clients with $100,000 in investible assets in his TV ads. Guess who walked through the door? People with $100,000 in investible assets. A week later, he advertised to those with $300,000 in investible assets. Guess what? Those with $300,000 in investable assets came knocking.

The picture you paint of your ideal client doesn't have to solely focus on money or investible assets either. Target markets are also identified by gender, age, political affiliation, and other characteristics. A sixty-year-old man with no family or house payment will respond to a different message than a young couple with three kids and a mortgage. A political conservative will respond to a different message than someone with no political affiliation.

Once you identify your ideal client, tailor the message to them and get that message out through the correct marketing funnel. A conservative radio show attracts conservatives. A radio show discussing family values attracts listeners interested in family. However you decide to identify your target market, if you do it correctly, you'll have more calls, more leads, and much better appointments.

However you decide to identify your target market, if you do it correctly, you'll have more calls, more leads, and more appointments.

One of the quickest ways to paint your ideal client is to survey top clients about their interests. How old are they? How much money have they saved? What do they value? What are they passionate about? What are their hobbies? Which political party do they identify with? What are their biggest concerns right now? One of my clients calls this his "What's in Your Head" survey. Use what's in the heads of your top clients to attract new ones that are just like them.

Attract ideal clients by following these steps:

1.) What do I do best? What problems do I best solve? What is fun business for me, what is profitable business for me? It starts with you. Identify this first.

2.) Look at your past clients—which ones have you enjoyed the most? Why? What characteristics do these clients share? Business owners? Churchgoers? Work in a certain region? Certain political views? Farmers?

3.) What challenges, concerns, fears do they share? What types of solutions were you able to help them with?

4.) Now you know what type of work you should do, what concerns you should address, and talk about in your marketing.

You have to constantly be engaged with your clients. You've got to listen to them. You can never get so big that you stop listening to each and every one of them.

One advisor, Brad, met with retirees about different types of investments. After a few marketing efforts, he noticed his potential clients were more concerned with whether they were going to run out of money than they were about getting a strong return on their investments. Brad listened to what his potential clients were saying, thought about it, and changed his marketing strategy completely. Instead of talking about estate planning and investments in his marketing materials, he started talking about income planning.

Brad didn't change what he was selling. In fact, one of his biggest strengths was how well he helped people with income planning. He just didn't advertise it on the front end. He didn't trick the clients. He didn't compromise his company's end goal. He simply changed his message. Guess what? His marketing response increased, and his sales process became easier. He spoke directly to his strengths and the audience's interest. As a result, his case size and business tripled.

The more congruent your marketing is, the less pressure you put on your sales process. Bring prospects in for the wrong reasons, and it's difficult to convince them you can help. Bring them in for the right reasons, and the sales process is easy.

> ## The more congruent your marketing is, the less pressure you put on your sales process.

When it comes to congruent marketing, good marketers use a rifle, not a shotgun. The shotgun approach brings people in for eight different things. This doesn't work because it doesn't support your end game and it doesn't help the client. Be a rifle. Find one topic, focus, and drive it home hard. A strong topic with a clearly driven point is much more impactful than eight, five minute segments about random topics. Sometimes the more you say, the less prospects remember. You want them walking away with a clear view of what you covered, not a cloudy memory of "what was this or that again?" There cannot be any surprises. You need to attract people based on how you can best help them. Be consistent, spread the correct message, cut to the chase, and you'll do more business.

Chapter 7: Speak Your Clients' Language

Make the most out of your marketing budget by:

1) Using a survey to profile your ideal client

2) Only marketing what you do best

3) Developing a message that supports your skillset and targets your ideal client

8

KNOW YOUR NUMBERS

"Before it can be solved, a problem
must be clearly defined."
— *William Feather*

W e've talked about investing in marketing and developing marketing goals, but that isn't enough to succeed in this business. Too many advisors set great goals and invest heavily in marketing but fail because they don't really know their numbers. They may have a good guess, but they are not precise.

To identify weak spots, look at your data and make decisions based on what you find. The data will tell you what steps in the process need to be improved, and then you can focus on those steps to improve your funnels.

You wouldn't play darts blindfolded. Don't do the same with marketing. You've got to know your numbers. Know your numbers! Know your numbers! Know your numbers!

Track More, Grow More

Many financial advisors put money in but never bother watching what comes out. They approach marketing by crossing their fingers and hoping for the best. The key to doubling or tripling business requires assessing marketing numbers, measuring outcomes, and making educated decisions based on existing data. Top advisors constantly monitor their marketing data. Guess what? The better they track that data, the more successful they are.

We get so busy going from appointment to appointment and event to event we don't realize that if we slowed down for a moment and looked at our numbers, the answers to our biggest problems would be crystal clear.

Another reason we often ignore our numbers is that margins in this business are relatively large, which is a blessing and a curse. Sales are so profitable that a few good ones meet your needs. Advisors have the possibility of tripling their money within six to eight weeks. Why worry about the details? Think about this. There are a lot of big businesses that must know their numbers inside and out. Take, for example, insurance companies that offer the products most agents and advisors use. Often times, these companies don't move into the black until three to four years after a policy is placed due to frontloaded costs.

Good margins are luxuries that can hide a multitude of sins. Namely, good margins allow you to ignore details that really need attention. Ignoring the details makes it impossible to know which buttons to push and levers to pull when it's time to grow your business, fix a problem, or evolve with the industry. You may make a change that works, but eventually, if you ignore the little details and lose touch with your numbers, production will languish. You'll become frustrated with the money going in and lack of progress coming out.

Real growth requires constant, intimate knowledge of the *correct* marketing numbers. For example, if seminar turnout is bad, the kneejerk response might be to stop seminars altogether based on *turnout numbers* and say they flat out don't work. However, a detailed look at seminar funnel data might indicate a positive return on investment (ROI) despite the low response rate. The big picture is ROI. The little numbers serve as diagnostics that show exactly what you need to do to improve.

Think of these little details as pieces of the dashboard on your car. Every one has a purpose. Every one tells you something about each of your funnels. The dashboard helps direct the adjustments and tweaks that will increase ROI over time. The dashboard helps navigate toward your goals.

In this business, we have the luxury of hindsight, but too many people don't use it. They make decisions based on a hunch or best guess. If you track your numbers—in detail—you'll know which funnels are working and which are not.

How to Feel Good about Marketing Spending

Because it's likely that each of your funnels will have different results, you must track them separately. Log how much radio ads cost, the number of calls they produce, and the number of appointments and clients they generate. What's the average case size and closing ratio based on the appointments that funnel generated? Go through the same exercise for seminars and direct mail. One funnel may produce higher net worth clients and larger case sizes, but may also create more difficult leads and lower closing ratios. Another might have a higher closing ratio, but a lower average case size. One may create a lot of leads that are nothing but time wasters. Regardless, you must know these numbers inside and out.

Analyzing the data from each funnel shows which marketing channels are the most effective, which need more resources, which need improvement, and which should be discontinued. These details are impossible to discern if you lump all marketing numbers into one big pot. You have to know every detail for each funnel.

It doesn't matter what your gut says; it doesn't matter how much feedback you get from seminar attendees. The only thing that matters is what the numbers say.

Take a look at how we tracked seminar numbers for my advisor, Kevin. Kevin was a $5 million producer with a goal of producing $8 million. Because seminars comprised the bulk of Kevin's marketing efforts, we looked at seminar numbers first. Ultimately, we wanted to know the effectiveness of his seminars, which means we had to know his seminar ROI. If you don't know ROI, it's impossible to determine the effectiveness of your marketing. It doesn't matter what your gut says; it doesn't matter how much feedback you get from seminar attendees. The only thing that matters is what the numbers say.

Take a look at this breakdown we did for Kevin.

KEVIN'S SEMINAR DATA

Mailers	8,000
RSVPs	80
Seminar attendees	70
Households	42
Appointments set	10
Appointments attended	7
Clients	3

While the above numbers are valuable, every assessment of marketing funnel data must also include average case size, average revenue per client, and the cost/value of the funnel. You should really know the acquisition cost of a client, cost per lead, and many other numbers as well. There are many numbers to know just to accurately assess one funnel.

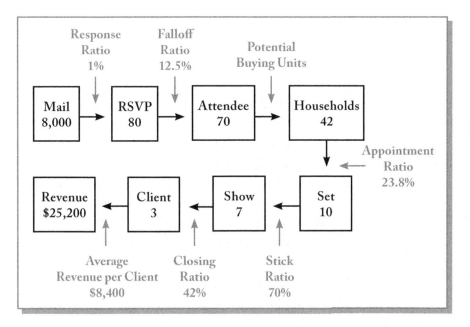

For Kevin, we next had to determine the value of his clients. Using a 5 percent commission rate, Kevin's clients had an average of $168,000 to invest. Therefore, each client was worth $8,400. For three clients, that's a total of $25,200.

$$\text{Mailers } \$0.70 \times 8,000\ (\$5,600)$$
$$\underline{+ \text{ the cost of the seminar } (\$2,500)}$$

$$\$8,100$$

Then, we had to weigh the total cost of marketing, which included mailers $5,600 ($.70 X 8,000) plus the cost of the seminar, $2,500, for a total of $8,100.

Doing some quick number crunching, this shows that for Kevin, seminars had an ROI of 3:1, which is pretty good. I have advisors who freak out when a funnel ratio decreases, but when that happens, you have to look at the ratio, not the decrease. I mean, where else can you get a 3:1 return on your money?

While 3:1 is pretty good, every process has a weakness. We wanted to identify Kevin's seminar weaknesses, which was possible once we knew his numbers.

We simply started from the top and worked our way down.

First, did Kevin's marketing get enough of a response to fill the room? The capacity of the room allowed for forty people a night. As you can see, an 8,000-piece mailer generated a response from eighty people. From that standpoint, it looks like the mailer did its job, right?

It's important to note here that some people make a huge mistake in terms of capacity. They schedule two nights for seminars, but only fill the room at half capacity. I've heard a lot of advisors convince themselves that this is the right approach. They'll say smaller groups are more intimate and impactful. However, I heard Tony Robbins speak and move an audience of more than 1,000, and then I saw him do a similar presentation in front of 100 people. He was clearly uncomfortable with the smaller group, yet a lot of people complain that 100 is too big. This experience changed my perspective. I no longer buy into the theory that a smaller group is better. It's just a matter of the advisor's comfort zone, not the audiences.

Think about it this way. Say you speak for an hour. Would you prefer to see twelve people and book three appointments with a 25 percent appointment ratio, or would you prefer to see thirty people and book six appointments for a 20 percent appointment-setting ratio? In this example, one hour of work either gets you six appointments or three appointments. Your time is worth something, and you get the highest ROI on your time when you talk to more people. So even if you have a higher conversion rate with a smaller audience, you're still better off speaking to more people.

Your time is worth something, and
you get the highest ROI on your
time when you talk to more people.

Too many advisors host multiple events every month that are half full. We had to make sure Kevin wasn't talking to a half-full room every month instead of filling one event once every other month. This approach gets similar results in less time. I'd much rather you spend time filling one room than hosting two rooms that are half full.

One of my elite advisors says that if sending 7,000 mailers results in a half-full room, send 14,000 mailers. It's not rocket science. Mail more people and fill the room.

Squash Buyer's Remorse and No-Shows

While we were looking at Kevin's seminar attendee numbers, we found another problem with Kevin's approach. Ten of the eighty people who RSVP'd didn't show up. They took the time to call and register, but something happened before the seminar that changed their mind.

For Kevin, we had to figure out how to interrupt that normal cycle of buyer's remorse. What could he do to not only confirm audience attendance, but also motivate them so they wouldn't back out? After crunching the numbers, we found Kevin had forty-two prospects at the seminar, which generated three new clients. So for every fourteen prospects in attendance, Kevin had one new client. With ten cancelling, Kevin lost at least five prospects. For a guy who does tons of seminars each year, this was a costly mistake. After every three seminar mailers, Kevin lost a client due to waste. Once the problem was exposed, we were able to go in and fix it.

We suggested Kevin have a representative from his company—someone who is friendly and speaks with confidence—call clients between when they agree to attend and the date of the event. Technically, this could be a prequalification call, but the intent is to get the right person influencing and exciting the prospect for the event. Kevin's key staff person made these calls, thanked prospects for RSVP'ing, and let them know how excited she was to meet them. She asked that they personally introduce themselves to her when they arrived. She then asked what they hoped to learn at the seminar, and said their input would impact the evening's discussion, which it did. This change alone excited people, made them feel more special, and boosted their confidence that their questions would be answered at the seminar. They also knew the topics they wanted to learn about would be discussed.

Guess what? This change alone decreased Kevin's cancellations and no show rate by an average of 50 percent. An action that only cost a fraction of one employee's time got Kevin approximately two-and-a-half more prospects in the audience.

Next, we moved onto appointments set. Getting 25 percent of prospects to set an appointment is okay; however, if Kevin wanted to improve the booking, he could boost the quality of his content. Maybe his PowerPoint slides were boring, he wasn't engaging, or his close wasn't moving enough. Each of these are small problems that are easily fixed with the right amount of focus and council.

We suggested that Kevin carefully analyze how he opens and closes his events and then learn from a professional how to drive his audience to action. This takes time, of course, but Kevin committed to studying what others were doing. Over time, this tactic made a difference.

Next, we noticed only seven of the ten appointments Kevin scheduled actually attended the meeting. Just because someone signs up for something doesn't mean they're going to attend. Potential clients will use every excuse possible not to attend. You have to stop these excuses before they start. For every seven appointments Kevin held, he got three clients, which is a closing ratio of 42 percent. If Kevin had kept the three that fell off, he would have had one more client per event, which is a revenue boost of $8,400. Fixing this one problem would increase his ROI to 4:1.

Let's first understand the situation in more detail. If your data shows a big drop off between the number of people who set an appointment and those who actually show up, find out why set appointments are lost. What happens? Do they cancel? Are they no-shows? Then, focus on finding a way to get those appointments to stick going forward.

Get into the head of your consumer. They loved your message and are excited to set an appointment. They take the time to call, or "opt in," but then a few days pass. Excitement fades and it fades fast. When a prospect books an appointment, they're engaged and focused because the appointment is at the forefront of their mind. That emotional high dissipates after a few days. Life happens, doubts creep in, and something else rises on their list of priorities. Before you know it, the appointment is canceled. Motivation diminishes with each day that goes by. What can you do to interrupt that process and re-excite the prospect?

We found that Kevin was pushing his appointments out three weeks. He had other priorities, and "filled" appointment slots as they were available. Kevin didn't think he needed to grab his prospects' attention while he was fresh in their minds. He didn't realize what a big deal this was.

The best advisors strike while the iron is hot. Appointments must be scheduled within seven days of when the client was empowered to make the appointment. Meet with prospective clients while interest is elevated, before the prospect loses the momentum riding on that emotional high. Timing is everything. Meeting within seven days also ensures that the information you discussed remains in the prospect's mind, which leads to better appointments.

The best advisors strike while the iron is hot. Appointments must be scheduled within seven days of when the client was empowered to make the appointment.

Kevin fixed his appointment issue by blocking enough time off on his calendar to ensure he met with every prospect within seven days. After spending so much money to get prospects to the seminar, Kevin didn't want their excitement to fade. Kevin succeeded in making sure his appointments trumped everything else.

During this process, Kevin made one more change. He interrupted the "motivation cycle." Most prospects set the appointment, a few days go by, and they don't hear much from the company.

To interrupt this cycle, Kevin sent his prospects a professional package that included a bio, a nice DVD about the firm, and a handwritten sticky note asking the prospect to view the DVD about his firm. He did this the day after the appointments were scheduled. Kevin interrupted the motivation cycle, wowed clients by going over the top, and thereby motivated his clients to see him.

Each package cost about $7 plus shipping, but decreased the chances of a client falling off big time. Interrupting Kevin's motivation cycle cost $70 ($7 X 10). The cost of his seminars increased by about 1 percent.

If implementing these tips saves two appointments out of the three that fell off, advisors almost always get a new client. In Kevin's case, spending $70 yielded an additional $8,400. What's the ROI on that?

By delving into Kevin's seminar numbers for ten minutes, we found numerous ways to improve his process. I've done this exercise multiple times with multiple advisors and have witnessed how small tweaks here or there can increase the net return on marketing funnels by thirty to fifty percent. But had we not known the problems within the funnel, we wouldn't have known what needed to be fixed. The biggest problems oftentimes are the biggest opportunities for your business, but they have to be exposed.

The biggest problems oftentimes are the biggest opportunities for your business, but they have to be exposed.

I've had producers tell me seminars don't work, only to find after a little data analysis that they make a 5:1 ROI on seminars and should actually be doing *more* of them. I've seen the same pattern with other funnels. You may think your radio show is a huge expense that isn't working. Yet after some number crunching, you may find that one year of the show yielded five clients who generated a great ROI for the funnel.

Consistently tracking and analyzing numbers will unveil 90 percent of the things you need to do to double or triple your business. Collect the data from each of your marketing funnels, realize the true ROI of each, and invest more in the most profitable funnels. Keep a close eye on your funnels, know what does and does not work, and make little tweaks that can lead to breakthroughs!

Chapter 8: Know Your Numbers

Want to double your business? Take a look at your numbers.

1) Crunch the numbers for each of your funnels

2) Decide which funnels need more resources, which need improvement, and which should be discontinued

3) Choose one funnel that needs improvement, and develop an action plan for improving that funnel

9

EVOLVE YOUR MARKETING STRATEGY

"What's dangerous is not to evolve."
— *Jeff Bezos*

We may not always think about a house's foundation—it isn't flashy, it's way beneath all the cool stuff, maybe it's hidden by some awesome landscaping—but without a foundation, everything else collapses. The same goes for your marketing strategy.

Build a Strong Foundation

Your marketing is the foundation of your business. If you don't have a strong foundation, it doesn't matter how fancy your other features are. Once the foundation is strong, think about pillars that hold up your roof. Each pillar represents a different funnel. The bigger your house, the more pillars you need. The more pillars you have, the more stable your roof. However, if any one pillar is weak, the whole roof could cave in. We just showed you how to crunch your numbers and how important it is to make them airtight. Build one pillar, make sure it's airtight, and then think about adding another.

Think of *The Money Pit*, the movie where a young couple buys a gorgeous mansion that's a total disaster. The doors fall off, the chimney collapses, and the floor is a minefield. Whoever built the house never perfected one thing before moving on to another. If you do not perfect the details of your funnels, expect *The Money Pit* nightmare. Unfortunately, your nightmare will damage your livelihood and nail a stake through those goals you set for your business.

Advisors with the best marketing strategies build strong foundations. First, they lay the groundwork, then they develop funnels that support congruent messages and speak to their ideal client. Next, they master one funnel—they know the numbers inside and out and get it to a point where the funnel runs with ease—before moving on to another. They let their marketing strategy evolve. They understand that no matter how strong the house, investing in adjustments, improvements, and general maintenance keeps the roof strong over time.

Constantly stay on top of your marketing numbers, but as you evolve and grow, learn to diversify. You don't want a business that is dependent on one strategy. No matter which funnels you use, over time, every funnel reaches a point of diminishing returns. Appointments booked entirely upon one marketing funnel are an invitation to professional Russian roulette. If it falls, the house falls.

We all believe we have the best products and services to offer. Because we don't want to be the best kept secret in town, we market.

Say the first time a wonderful idea is marketed, it goes to 1,000 people. The response rate is 5 percent. Not bad. The next time, the response rate is 3 percent. Over time, the response rate trickles to 1 percent. This response rate trickle happens with every single funnel. The more you market—and the more others in your area market—the lower your return. Even if you hit a winning formula, it's only a matter of time before that marketing strategy has to change or evolve. Your opportunity to capitalize on your winning formula diminishes little by little. The more you invest in your funnels, the greater advantage you can take of marketing opportunities that work today.

Know When to Keep and When to Ditch Marketing Methods

Over the last ten years, I've seen diminishing returns work with a variety of funnels. Years ago, direct mail was an extremely effective funnel for generating appointments. You could send a mail piece, high quality prospects would request information or come see you, and response rates hit 2–3 percent. Today, the same strategy yields a response rate of less than .5 percent, and the quality of responders is lower. This funnel is no longer profitable on its own. When this happens—when a funnel becomes routine—it's no longer new. It reaches a point of diminishing returns.

I had a Texas advisor who worked in a fairly small city test this direct mail approach to seminars. The first time he used direct mail, the response rate was 3.4 percent. At the time, the industry average for direct mail was about 1 percent. His 3.4 percent was pretty good and likely related to the market being fairly virgin to this approach. A couple months later, the advisor's response rate hit 3 percent. Over time, it trickled to 2 percent and then fell in line with the industry standards at about 1 percent.

The funny thing is, this advisor called me when response rates dropped to 2 percent. He was upset and wanted to quit using direct mail. I told him his efforts were twice as effective as the industry average and then explained diminishing returns. The advisor seized the day and kept using direct mail.

The same thing happens with seminars, but that doesn't mean they're ineffective. The effectiveness of seminars differs from advisor to advisor. Use your numbers to determine whether seminars still work for you. The total return on your money may have been 8:1 when you started, but a 3:1 return is still pretty good. In fact, one of my top producers does a lot of national advertising. He spends so much money and hits the marketing so hard, that he only expects to get a 1.5:1 return on his money. That would seem bad in comparison to an advisor making 3:1, but if my advisor spends $10 million or more on his marketing, he nets $5 million in revenue. It still works for him. You have to decide what works best for you, but where else can you make 50 percent on your money? Like we saw before, to figure out your ROI, you have to know your numbers. If you don't, you'll have no idea how to change your marketing strategy when diminishing returns occur.

You always want a few funnels working simultaneously because marketing funnels work like bike spokes. If one spoke breaks, the wheel still turns until the broken funnel is fixed or replaced. For ultimate success, you want a few funnels working simultaneously. Once the funnels start working together, they function so well, it's sometimes difficult to immediately determine which one is creating results.

> You always want a few funnels working simultaneously because marketing funnels work like bike spokes. If one spoke breaks, the wheel still turns until the broken funnel is fixed or replaced.

For example, I had an advisor who asked a client why he attended a seminar. The advisor assumed his attendance was motivated by something on the seminar invite. He was wrong. The client said he had been listening to the advisors radio show for quite some time. He enjoyed the show, so when the seminar invite showed up the mail, he decided to attend. Both funnels worked together to increase the efficiency of the advisor's overall marketing efforts. The advisor's congruent marketing strategy was effective. And by the way, his radio show wasn't just branding like we spoke about before. It also generated appointments consistently so he got the effects of branding for free.

Avoid Dry Spells

Without exception, elite advisors have multiple, diversified marketing funnels working simultaneously. It doesn't happen overnight. Elite advisors master one funnel and then move on and master a second. First, they test the funnel. Then, they optimize it. Before long, they master it and it becomes a major part of their business. No one funnel will ever break their business because they have so much business coming in from different funnels.

Producers solely reliant on seminars, radio shows, or any other single marketing funnel, are essentially hopping around on pogo sticks. Unfortunately, when one funnel topples, business does, too.

To free your business from depending on one marketing funnel, constantly test new and better funnels. I recommend setting aside 10 percent of your marketing budget for test funnels. This test budget will help you gradually develop additional pillars. Before you know it, you'll have three to five pillars working together to support your business.

Like most things in this business, testing a new funnel doesn't mean reinventing the wheel. Before testing a new funnel, talk to five advisors who have tried a similar funnel. What were the results? What lessons did they learn?

Research and develop your marketing strategy, talk to people already using those funnels for tips on best practices, pull the trigger, and add that funnel to your overall marketing strategy.

Marketing ROI Over Time

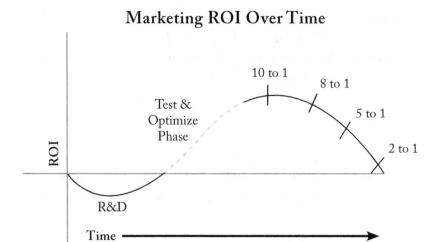

Warning: Do not ditch your entire marketing plan just to try a new one. This can derail the progress you've already made.

Here's an example of how big changes to your marketing strategy can destroy your business. Years ago, I worked with a brilliant top advisor named Jack. He did $8 million to $10 million a year. His marketing plan was working (obviously) but he wanted to try something new. Instead of keeping his current marketing strategy while testing new funnels, he ditched his current marketing strategy and went with the new, untested strategy. He viewed the new shiny object marketing approach as a replacement for what was working instead of as a supplement. It didn't go well. In fact, Jack's production dropped by half and he ended up scrambling to figure out what went wrong.

Top producers have multiple, diversified marketing funnels. If one funnel fails one week, another produces appointments. Because these advisors are less dependent on a single funnel to meet their business needs, they rarely have dry spells. They have mature, well-developed businesses.

Top producers have multiple, diversified marketing funnels. If one funnel fails one week, another produces appointments. Because these advisors are less dependent on a single funnel to meet their business needs, they rarely have dry spells.

There are tons of marketing concepts common to other industries, but foreign to ours. These ideas might be game changers, but exposure must be slow. Learn them, add them to your business over time and decide if they belong with your company. If your test concept is a win, gradually turn up the volume and add that technique as another pillar. Do not replace a current strategy with a new one. Going all in is for poker, not business.

B   O   A   R   D

Chapter 9: Evolve Your Marketing Strategy

Take a look at your funnels and ask yourself the following:

1) How many marketing funnels do I currently use in my business?

2) What new funnels could I add to my practice?

3) Whom do I know that utilizes that funnel currently that I could learn from?

10

ROCKET FUEL YOUR BUSINESS

"Investing is laying out money now to
get more money back in the future."
— *Warren Buffet*

I f this isn't poker and you're not all in, how do you know how much to spend on marketing? Get your head around fixed costs and fuel costs.

Fixed costs include overhead—rent and support staff salaries— and do not change as a function of the business. You know what they are and pay them monthly or annually. Fuel costs, on the other hand, are marketing-related expenses that fuel appointments and business. This is an important distinction because fuel costs are often mistakenly listed as expenses and are therefore hacked during budget cuts. But why would you cut a cost that makes money and has a great ROI—3:1, 4:1, 5:1—depending on the funnel?

When it comes to expenses, advisors often throw marketing in with fixed costs. Unfortunately, when it's budget-cutting time, marketing is the first to go. Advisors panic and slash costs without considering the cost and benefit of each. They hack seminars because they can be expensive and difficult to run. On paper, eliminating a seminar or two shows a reduction in cost. Money saved, right? Not necessarily.

Are You Slashing or Propelling Future Growth?

As we touched on earlier, your single biggest business cost isn't what you are doing, it's what you aren't doing. It isn't a fixed cost. It's the opportunity cost of marketing less than you should be. Marketing fuels business. Cutting that fuel supply will destroy your engine. In fact, for every $1 you cut your fuel costs by, your business might lose $3, $4, or $5 in future revenue.

Let's take a look by reverse engineering our numbers. Let's say an advisor makes one sale for every five first appointments. For this advisor, an average sale is $250,000 with total earnings for the business at $15,000. In this scenario, every first appointment is worth $3,000 ($15,000 per new case / five appointments to get one case = $3,000 per appointment). This advisor generates $3,000 in revenue every time a new appointment is scheduled and kept.

Assume the same advisor spends $7,000 to conduct and fill a seminar. Costs include the mailer, food, room, and miscellaneous expenses. Let's assume every seminar leads to an average of ten first appointments with qualified prospects. For this example, each first appointment costs $700 to acquire. To reach that number, simply divide the $7,000 in costs by the ten appointment generated.

Remember, the advisor earns $3,000 in revenue for each first appointment. After factoring in marketing expenses, that's a net profit of $2,300 per appointment generated ($3,000 per first appointment - $700 in marketing cost = $2,300 net profit).

To calculate total earnings from the event, consider ten first appointments at $3,000 per first appointment, which is $30,000 in revenue. Subtract the $7,000 seminar cost, and net profit yields $23,000.

For each of the ten first appointments made and kept, business increases by $2,300. If just one appointment is missed, there's a revenue loss of $3,700. The $3,000 in revenue for the first appointment plus the $700 it cost to get the appointment.

The Real Cost of Cutting Marketing

For every seminar not conducted, the loss is ten new appointments. A seminar that would have cost $7,000 ends up costing

$23,000 in future net revenue that was missed. Therefore, cutting fuel costs and reducing marketing actually costs more than hosting the seminar.

As long as your marketing strategy works, your biggest business cost is the invisible cost of not having appointments in the first place. Sticking with the previous example, every week without five first appointments is a loss of $15,000. Three empty spots in the calendar where first appointments should be cost $9,000 in revenue. That's more than it would have cost to host a seminar.

> As long as your marketing strategy works, your biggest business cost is the invisible cost of not having appointments in the first place.

If you don't have enough first appointments on your calendar, fuel your marketing budget, and keep that calendar filled. Without enough rocket fuel, your business will never reach the heights you've set for it.

B O A R D

Chapter 10: Rocket Fuel Your Business

Think about cutting your expenses. Before you do, answer the following:

1) What are my fixed costs?

2) What are my fuel costs?

3) What is one appointment worth to my business?

11

BE A FARMER AND A HUNTER

"Successful people do what unsuccessful people refuse to do. Don't wish it were easier, wish you were better."

— Jim Rohn

When your marketing is in full force, you'll have an opportunity to see lots of people over time. Some of them will become clients, some will not. Take seminars as an example. Think of all the people who attended your seminar, but didn't set an appointment. What if you did ten seminars? What about 100? No matter how good you are, a lot of people will either not set an appointment with you, or will set one, but not become a client. The people who don't buy initially are often times left alone and end up falling through the cracks. But with a little bit of focus and effort, that list of people can actually become one of your greatest assets.

Many advisors approach clients with a hunter mentality of capturing whatever comes across their path. It's an immediate gain. Farmers take a different approach. They spend years growing and cultivating crops. It's a less immediate approach, but it still yields great results. The most successful advisors at Advisors Excel are farmers *and* hunters.

Know "No" Isn't Forever

If an advisor has a 30 percent closing ratio, seven out of ten people they meet with *will not* become a client. If that same advisor meets with 100 clients a year, seventy of them *will not* become clients. If an advisor hosts a seminar for forty people four times a month, she sees 160 people a month. During the course of a year, that puts the advisor in front of 1,920 people. Half book an appointment, the other half does not, so that advisor only continues the relationship with 960 of 1,920 people.

Advisors spend so much time and money sharing their message, yet when prospects don't buy, they move onto the next client without looking back. This is one of the biggest and most common mistake advisors make because it leaves a large list of potential buyers sitting by the side of the road.

As good as your marketing is, it's not perfect. You cannot capitalize on every opportunity because your opportunities are people. Every day these people are affected by outside factors that are out of your control. They may not be able to work with you at one specific moment in time for numerous reasons. The hard part was getting them to pop their head up. Once they do, why not stay in touch?

My advisor, Tom, taught me a very important lesson about this. Like everyone else, Tom built his business by hunting new prospects. He used different funnels to generate leads, and he let prospects who didn't become clients fall off his radar. Eventually, Tom thought about the thousands of people he had met with over the years. He decided to put some energy into nurturing that list of people by reconnecting with them.

Think about it. Tom meets Sally at a seminar. Sally learns a lot and enjoys Tom's message, but the timing isn't right so she doesn't set an appointment. Tom adds Sally to his "future prospects list" and stays in touch from time to time. He adds her to his thought of the week email and client newsletter. He even invites her to an event from time to time when extra room is available. Within a year, Sally calls Tom out of the blue. She tells Tom she's ready to retire and would like to talk about a 401(k). Tom hardly remembers Sally, but Sally remembers Tom because he stayed in touch.

Avoid the Out-of-Sight, Out-of-Mind Trap

Reverse this scenario. Say Tom never stayed in touch. Eventually, when Sally decides she needs help, she doesn't think of Tom because he hasn't stayed at the forefront of her mind. Instead, she turns to the Internet and Googles "financial advisor, Utah." Tom doesn't get the business. He is out of sight and out of mind.

Tom says he's a hunter like everybody else, but unlike everyone else, he's also a farmer. When he plants seeds (prospects) he nurtures them over time. Eventually, when they're ready, they bloom into a nice harvest.

Tom has a database of more than 1,200 people who aren't currently clients. The amount of time, effort, and money it takes to keep in touch with those prospects is minimal.

Most advisors are too busy to realize losing touch with prospects is like letting money fall through the cracks. Your list of prospects has extreme value. Even when they don't buy, stay in touch by dripping on them. When they're ready, you'll be the first advisor they call. You spend so much money meeting prospects. Stay in touch so they think of you when the timing is better for them.

Find the Riches in Your Current Database

The concept of being a farmer *and* a hunter has been proven as a sustainable business generator time and time again. One advisor, who logs $40 million per year in new assets, gets $12 million annually from his current prospects database. Think about that: 30 percent of his business comes from his database, which was developed by keeping in touch with the "nos" and "maybes."

The farming concept can be applied to every single funnel. Create a database of seminar attendees, radio callers, and people who contact the office, but then decline your service. They may not be ready to say yes now, but that doesn't mean they won't be ready in a week, month, or year.

Tom shared this lesson, which I'll never forget. He said, "If you have high-priority prospects you'd like to have as clients, treat them as if they already are, and over time, they will be."

No truer words have been spoken. Think about it. If your team is constantly bringing value to these prospects by updating them with important information, they will eventually become your clients.

Another thing Tom gets is timing. He knows that by staying in touch, he will be the first call prospects make when things change and they're in need of a financial advisor. It may not happen for a month, or even a year, but when the situation changes, Tom's their man.

Too often advisors label someone who attends a seminar, but doesn't make an appointment, a plate licker when in reality, their current life circumstance might not allow for a new investment. But what happens when the market drops, or they feel their current advisor has let them down, or they have a CD due?

One of my advisor's clients decided against an appointment after his seminar. The prospect had just changed advisors and didn't want to change again. Okay, no problem. The advisor stayed in touch and sent valuable information to the prospect while she worked with her existing advisor. Six months later, the woman called. The market was down, she was losing, and the new advisor who was so nice and charming six months ago, wouldn't return her calls. Finally, she was ready to work with someone new. My advisor was her top pick. When she called my advisor, she said, "You communicate with me more than my advisor does, so why wouldn't I work with you?"

Things change all the time. Someone planning to retire in six months gets offered his dream job; an inheritance unexpectedly comes through; a relationship falls apart. The point is, you never know what's behind any decision to pass on doing business with you. It's your job to make sure you're the first person that prospect calls when their situation changes.

B O A R D

Chapter 11: Be a Farmer and a Hunter

Don't let a single prospect fall through the cracks.

1) Dig out contact information from prospects who decided not to do business with you

2) Add them to your drip list

3) Stay in touch in case things change, and find ways to bring value to them from time to time

12

UNDERSTAND THE VALUE OF AN APPOINTMENT

"I don't qualify people with my
marketing efforts, I disqualify them."
— *Elite Advisor, IL*

I worked with an advisor a few years back who was struggling. When I asked why, he said, "I'm just too busy." I then asked where he spent the majority of his time. He said, "Meeting with people."

We analyzed his meetings, paying close attention to the types of meetings he set. One was a lunch with a friend who he hoped to talk business with. Another was with a woman who was interested in talking to him, but wouldn't make a financial decision without her husband, who wasn't there. One was a referral—a client's son—who was interested in term life insurance.

Good appointments require meeting with interested decision makers who:

- Fall within your target market

- Align with your goals and values
- Are highly motivated and interested in what you do best
- Are able to make a decision

Having people come in for term life insurance, when that's not something you offer, is a waste of time and so is speaking to someone who isn't a decision maker.

Every appointment on your calendar has some value. You need to decide what it is.

Three Ways to Increase Sales Revenue

I learned a great lesson from an advisor who said that in this business, you can really only increase sales revenue one of three ways.

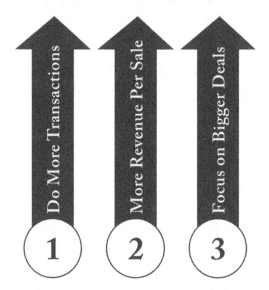

One, do more transactions every year. If you bring on 100 clients with $100,000 in new assets this year, next year bring on 200 clients and you'll double production.

Two, bring in more revenues per sale. In this instance, think about product. Instead of selling cell phones in the mall, sell cars. The margins are much higher. In our business, this might mean focusing on life insurance, which may average a couple of grand per sale, rather than medical supplements, which yield $100 per sale.

Three, focus on bigger deals. Say you bring on $100,000 clients per case. If you find and attract $200,000 clients per case, you could do the same number of transactions while also doubling your business. For example, one of my advisors only works with clients who have at least $1 million. He would rather give fewer clients a higher quality experience than have a high volume business. He can do more production in one month by bringing on one new client than most businesses can do by bringing on ten clients each month.

Stop Wasting Time with the Wrong Prospects

All three of these models require that you know the value of your appointments. Not all prospects are equal. Think about it. Effective marketing funnels attract the correct prospects while also filtering out the bad prospects. If your message attracts one person, it repels another. Ideal prospects surface while the others disappear.

Top advisors have businesses that are strategically designed to sound alarm bells when the wrong clients come knocking. In fact, one of my top advisors once said, "I don't qualify people with my marketing efforts, I disqualify them."

One of my top advisors once said,
"I don't qualify people with my
marketing efforts, I disqualify them."

He knows that he only wants the right people to see him, so he doesn't waste his time with people who aren't good candidates for the help he provides. He gets it. I totally agree.

Say three prospects who aren't likely candidates for what you do come to see you. You meet with them for a first appointment and talk yourself into thinking they might be a good fit for a second meeting. Then, after the second meeting, you schedule a third meeting with them. The entire time you're trying to fit a square peg in a round hole. You know they're not a good fit, but you want the sale so badly you keep trying to turn the prospect into something they are not.

In the meantime, at an hour an appointment, you've spent nine hours with the three of the wrong people. Wouldn't it be better to know after the first appointment if each prospect is a highly likely candidate? Then you spend three hours with them instead of nine. What if you realized they were a bad prospect before the first meeting? That's a savings of nine hours. Your goal should always be to fill your calendar with the *right* appointments.

Advisor A				
M	**TU**	**W**	**TH**	**F**
	Bad Prospect A 1-hr meeting #2		Bad Prospect C 1-hr meeting #2	
		Bad Prospect C 1-hr meeting #1		Bad Prospect B 1-hr meeting #3
	Bad Prospect B 1-hr meeting #1		Bad Prospect A 1-hr meeting #3	
Bad Prospect A 1-hr meeting #1		Bad Prospect B 1-hr meeting #2		Bad Prospect C 1-hr meeting #3

Advisor B				
M	**TU**	**W**	**TH**	**F**
		Bad Prospect C 1-hr meeting #1		
	Bad Prospect B 1-hr meeting #1			
Bad Prospect A 1-hr meeting #1				

Same result: Advisor A = 9 hours vs. Advisor B = 3 hours

Building a business with the mindset to serve anyone who can fog a mirror systematically sets the stage for a lifetime of migraines and mayhem. Not only does this apply to the services you provide, it applies to your company values. For example, if a prospect walks into the office, shakes your hand, and starts bragging about the money he can invest as a result of winning a lawsuit he waged against another business, step back. Does this person share your personal values? How about your company values? Do you really want to work with them?

Determining where to draw the line with a client is a personal decision. One advisor in Texas works in a gambling community, but refuses to work with gamblers. He feels their cash flow is unreliable in the short term and his expertise is best suited for people with a long-term time horizon. They have funds one day, and nothing the next. This advisor says, "a gambler's money never has a home" meaning they may invest now, but if they go on a bad run, they'll need their money immediately. Their so-called long-term view on investing changes due to chance. While this advisor is anti-gambling clients, plenty of financial advisors work with gamblers. Someone out there works with them. It's up to you to decide if that's your game. Who you do business with is a personal decision but, as Warren Buffet says, "You can't do *good* business with *bad* people."

In the context of the Buffet quote, who is good and who is bad is all about whether they are right for you.

Most producers don't identify their bad client type until it's too late. They ignore the alarm bells, enthusiastically bring on the client, and then six months later wish they hadn't. Maybe the bad client is high maintenance, arrogant, disrespectful to their spouse, or rude to a member of the team. Maybe they're impossible to work with, or just don't fit the company culture. Whatever the case, I've seen endless incidences where advisors would have paid twice the revenue they earned to get these bad clients off the books. In these instances, short-term opportunity leads to long-term headache.

Be Okay with Not Bringing on Everyone You Meet

When it comes to choosing clients, selectivity will lead to a healthier, more robust business. Your clients will sense that you enjoy working with them. They will appreciate that you aren't desperate for their business, and a lasting relationship developed on mutual respect will mature.

I can't tell you how many times I've heard an advisor pound his chest while rambling on about his 90 percent closing ratio. His message: I'm a great salesman. I bring on everyone I meet. Not only is this a false claim, if it were true, he'd have a miserable business. Great salespeople don't bring on everyone they meet. They don't want to, and they don't have to.

> Great salespeople don't bring on everyone they meet. They don't want to, and they don't have to.

Be okay with not having a 90 percent closing ratio. It's far better to stand on a stage smiling about how your brilliant marketing funnels weeded out bad clients than it is to have a 90 percent closing rate and a sore chest because you can't stand most of your clients.

Regardless of how you choose to increase business, know what every appointment is worth and choose who you do and do not want to do business with.

Chapter 12: Understand the Value of an Appointment

Stop wasting time with the wrong prospects, and start focusing on spending time with the right ones. Ask yourself:

1) What's the value of my appointments?

2) Which of the three strategies to increase revenue do I want to pursue?

3) How can I change my business model to reach that goal?

13

BE CONSISTENT AND PERSISTENT

"If you really want to do something, you'll find a way. If not, you'll find an excuse."

— Jim Rohn

op advisors never develop a marketing strategy and then let it come to a dead stop mid-year. They never say, "I can't do seminars in Florida in the summer because it's just too hot," or, "I can't do seminars in Michigan in the winter because it's just too cold." They don't make these excuses.

Standard marketing results will differ from month to month, but that doesn't mean you should shut down your marketing efforts completely because one month is slower than the next. In fact, it may mean those efforts need ramping up. A 7,000-piece mailing that normally fills the room may need to be a 10,000-piece mailing to generate the same results in the summer, but you're better off spending a little more on a larger mailing than going dark for two months.

Maximize Momentum with Minimal Effort

If you want to grow your business, learn to prime the pump. To use a Zig Ziglar analogy, imagine an old outdoor well and pump.

Priming that pump after it hasn't been primed for several weeks is exhausting. If the pump were primed every so often, water would flow much more easily. The same applies to marketing. If you stop the flow of prospects from a given well, starting it up again requires a lot of time and effort. Maintaining the flow and returning from time to time is much easier.

A few years ago, an advisor notorious for having low production during January asked if other advisors always started the year slowly. Sure, some advisors have a slow start, but this guy's January production was nonexistent. We looked through his marketing calendar. It didn't take long to see his production lagged because he stopped his marketing four to six weeks before the end of the year. He didn't market in November because he assumed people wouldn't want to meet in December. He stopped priming the pump.

> It's far more costly to stop-start marketing efforts than it is to occasionally boost efforts for four to eight weeks during a slow period.

The year following our conversation, the advisor marketed through December for the first time. His January was record breaking. Overall, his business was up more than 30 percent, a hike he attributes to priming that pump. The biggest factor in increasing his production was the addition of one month of marketing every year.

It's far more costly to stop-start marketing efforts than it is to occasionally boost efforts for four to eight weeks during a slow period. Advisors often think the lag time for restarting marketing efforts is three to four weeks, when it's often closer to six to seven weeks. For a forty five week a year business, a six to seven week lag multiple times a year is a dangerous proposition.

I once heard of an advisor who wanted to prove everyone wrong about "bad times to market," so he held a seminar on Thanksgiving night, filling a room with people who didn't have plans for a number of reasons. The point is, when you think it's a bad time to market, other advisors do, too. By stepping on the gas and marketing when most of your competitors are not, you win. Think of how little competition that advisor had for attendees at his Thanksgiving night seminar.

Your marketing strategy needs to be consistent regardless of weather, time of year, or funnel. My advisor, Brett, is a $6 million producer who has extreme swings in productivity. Brett isn't one of my "I don't market over the holidays," or "it's too hot to market in the summer" producers. In fact, he struggles with priming the pump in a different way. Every other month, Brett hosts a seminar and brings in about $1 million in new assets. These are his good months. During his down months, he does less than $100,000.

Brett's Monthly Production

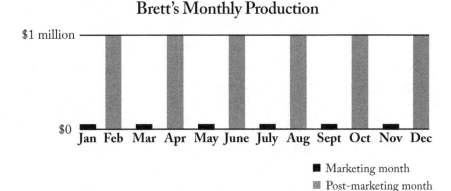

If Brett could fix the $100,000 troughs, he could bring in $12 million a year in new assets as opposed to $6 million. He could double his production.

We found that Brett's spurts of extreme productivity followed down months in which he was harvesting clients. For Brett, that meant conducting seminars. So his seminars were really effective, but when he was creating leads, he wasn't producing. Simply put, in January, Brett marketed for new clients and then spent the rest of January and February working with those prospects to convert them to clients. This led to a big production month in February. He then marketed in March, wrote business in April, and so on. Every other month he marketed, every other month he wrote business. He didn't do both consistently. So the answer for him to increase production was to do both consistently every month. Brett continued doing his seminars every other month. That was enough for him. However, he decided to add a weekly radio show to his business as another marketing funnel. The key here was that the radio show played every single week of the year. There were no off months. This forced him to market consistently. The result? That year, Brett wrote more than $12 million in production. That one change created a huge breakthrough for him. Another point here is that Brett planned his marketing a full year in advance. By having seminars and the radio show scheduled, he knew exactly where he was headed and never failed to follow through on those marketing efforts.

By planning your marketing calendar a year in advance like Brett did, you eliminate the possibility of failing to market. You get rid of the "should I, should I not" market this month dilemma. It's better to build out the full year worth of marketing because if it's on the calendar you have to do it. Another advisor that I work with recently did this and said it made a huge difference in his results. It gave him a schedule and he stuck to it.

Don't Become Your Own Worst Enemy

While you're working on filling those lulls in the calendar, do me a favor. Don't become your own worst enemy. If you come across a problem, solve it, and learn to be bigger than it. Here's an example. Last winter one of Advisor Excel's top producers called in a panic.

"Shawn," he said. "I've just lost an entire month's production."

I thought he must have been a victim of a technical meltdown or medical catastrophe. That wasn't the case. He was actually a victim of a blizzard. It covered his city and prevented anyone from attending that week's seminars. That same day, another advisor who lives twenty-five miles east of the first advisor also called. That advisor was totally excited. The same blizzard had ruined his seminar, yet he was going sledding. He had eight other events planned that month and so one cancellation was no big deal.

Diversifying marketing efforts and planning for inevitable hiccups such as blizzards or cancellations is critical to growth. If you only plan one seminar a month and that seminar is canceled for whatever reason, you lose a month's production. If, on the other hand, you plan eight seminars that month, one cancellation will not decimate production. The first advisor in this example was one hundred percent out of luck when that blizzard hit, while the second knew 80 percent of his marketing efforts would go forward as planned.

> Diversifying marketing efforts and planning for inevitable hiccups such as blizzards or cancellations is critical to growth.

The most successful advisors do not leave the success of their business vulnerable to small problems. They create so many other opportunities that they become bigger than any problem that may arise and end up outgrowing their problems all together.

Focus on proactively placing yourself in a position where you are bigger than your problems so you can handle whatever comes your way.

B   O   A   R   D

Chapter 13: Be Consistent and Persistent

To grow your business, constantly prime the pump by:

1) Committing to consistently marketing year-round

2) Planning your marketing calendar for a full year at a time

3) Refusing to leave your business vulnerable because it's based on one marketing strategy

SECTION 2:
MASTER MARKETING
SUMMARY

Marketing is an investment, not an expense. Without it, you have no way to contact clients or set appointments, which is the ultimate goal. Understand the difference between marketing and branding and invest heavily in diversifying marketing funnels.

Develop congruent, direct response marketing strategies that target your core audiences with messages that highlight your strengths. Never bait and switch prospects by offering to talk about something the client cares about, but something you know little about. Keep an eye on every single one of your funnels. Understand what the ROI is for each of your marketing funnels by knowing the numbers for each and every one. When a funnel's ROI decreases, look back through your numbers and determine why the ROI is on the decline, whether the funnel needs tweaking, or whether you need to introduce a new funnel altogether. Avoid lulls in your marketing strategy by diversifying your funnels, and always save 10 percent of your marketing budget for testing new funnels. Research new funnels before introducing them to your business. Never replace a current funnel that is working without testing the new funnel first, and consider the difference between fixed costs and fuel costs before you start cutting your expenses.

Staying in touch with prospects who do not set appointments by creating valuable drip lists will help grow your business. Send information to these prospects from time to time so that when things change and they need a financial advisor, they come to you. Know the value of each appointment, and focus on setting appointments with high value clients who share your personal values. Always remember that without marketing, you won't have any appointments, and without appointments, you don't have a business.

SUMMARY

Section 2: Master Marketing

Top Three GO Elite Actions to Master Marketing:

1) Know your numbers inside and out, and use them to adjust your marketing strategy

2) Let your marketing strategy evolve and diversify your funnels

3) Focus on setting appointments with the *right* prospects, and keep in touch with prospects by developing a good drip list

MASTER SALES

"Sales are contingent on the attitude of the salesman—not the attitude of the prospect."

— *W. Clement Stone*

Themhe first thing you need to learn about sales is that sales isn't about selling. It's not about magical phrases, the perfect close, or your ability to influence people. It's about helping people, solving problems, and adding value.

Unfortunately, the terms salesman and saleswoman often bring slick-haired, irritating, pushy professionals to mind. Rarely do clients see a salesman or saleswoman as the nice woman who suggested the perfect solution to their problem, or the realtor who found the perfect home. Instead, they imagine an uninformed suit with money symbols in their eyes and greed in their hearts. This is because many clients' only interactions with salespeople are negative.

Great salespeople aren't pushy or manipulative. Great salespeople are caring problem solvers who always approach a sale with the goal of adding tremendous value to their clients. They believe wholeheartedly in the difference they can make and are so sincere in this belief, they make sales look easy.

Great salespeople are empathetic toward their clients' wants, needs, and concerns. They go into every sale asking how they can best help their client, how they can rid them of pain and bring them pleasure. Perhaps a client's pain is that they don't have enough money to support their retirement goals. Pleasure, then, is solving the problem and developing a fantastic financial package that will allow them to retire while also giving them the confidence and certainty that retirement is something they'll no longer have to worry about.

Clients always have a concern, need, or perceived need—something on their mind that shakes their confidence, causes worry, or leads them to believe they could be better off. They share these private concerns with us because they hope we—or someone like us —will address them and put them in a more comfortable position financially. We have the ability to boost a client's confidence so that when they leave a meeting with us, they are in a better place than they were when they arrived.

When the top salespeople I've studied go into a sale, they don't think of it as a sale. They think of it as an opportunity to help someone by identifying a need and solving a problem. This requires developing the right attitude toward sales. It requires believing wholeheartedly in what you can do for the client and focusing on doing good rather than achieving outcomes.

OBJECTIVES

Section 3: Master Sales

In this section, you will learn how to:

- Ask clients questions that reach their emotional core
- Develop a dynamic personal story to better connect with your clients
- Sell the thing—package, service, team—that differentiates you from competitors
- Add value to clients at every turn
- Develop a six-step sales process
- Handle objections with ease
- Effectively and consistently close a sale
- Project an image that's consistent with the one you want to project

14

SELL TO SERVE

"You know you are on the road to success when you would do your job and not be paid for it."

— *Oprah*

Ten years ago, when I started in this business, I defined selling as influencing or persuading someone to take action. Working with the country's top advisors changed that, and quickly.

Selling isn't about convincing clients to take action. It isn't about making a commission, and it isn't about creating revenue. Selling is about making a difference, helping clients, and bettering people's lives.

Many advisors go into a sale with this mindset: "If I can close this, I'll make $2,000."

Honestly, this mindset is common when people start in this business. The most powerful position to be in is one where money doesn't drive the sale, when revenue received is the last thing you think about. This happens most often when advisors gain experience and have success.

Advisors understand that clients come to them because they have financial concerns. But advisors who understand who their clients are, what motivates them, and how they view themselves close far more sales than advisors who have basic knowledge of a client. No two clients are the same. How well you understand your client directly correlates to how much success you'll have with them.

Be a Good Listener: Understand Your Clients

Many of the most elite advisors *really* get to know their client. Instead of focusing on what they should tell the client, they focus on what the client can tell *them*. So many advisors don't realize they're failing because they can't beat a desire to talk all time. We have two ears and one mouth for a reason—the greatest salespeople use both by asking questions and being good listeners. This provides the empathy and understanding the advisor needs to really understand how to help the client.

This requires digging beyond basic fact-finding financial questions. Understand what money historically means to your client. Understand the impact existing financial concerns have on their family and quality of life. Ask the following questions, which were inspired by best-selling author Mitch Anthony. What does money represent to you? How much time in your life does this money represent? What sacrifices does money represent?

Top advisors know that to clients, money isn't just about money. They get a better understanding of the deeper meaning behind money and therefore have a much better understanding of the client, which leads to a stronger connection and, ultimately, more sales. Remember, your sales process is only as good as your understanding of your prospects, which depends entirely on the quality of the questions you ask.

DIGGING DEEPER

1) What does money represent to you?

2) How much time in your life does this money represent?

3) What sacrifices does money represent?

Ask Better Questions

One of my advisors, Alan, was struggling with his sales process and wanted to improve by watching another advisor run his appointments. One of my other advisors, Terry, who does a great job selling life insurance, volunteered to run some appointments with Alan and split some business. They ran appointments together for a couple days. It was a successful venture for both. However, the most valuable lesson Alan got from the experience had nothing to do with writing business. Alan brought existing clients in for appointments—people he'd been working with for years—to discuss how Terry's specialty in life insurance might help them. After the meeting, Alan called me and said, "Shawn, you won't believe this. The questions Terry asked and the way he ran the appointments, gave Terry more insight into my clients after one hour than I gained after years of working with them."

Terry's level of understanding clients requires phenomenal listening skills and great questions. What's your client's story? What do they like? What inspires them? What makes them tick? What's their first memory of money? This last question may sound odd question, but it gives historical insight into what influenced the client's perspective of money, which can lead to a better solution for that client. Not only does sharing meaningful insights allow for a better solution, it also deepens the bond with the client. Think about it. Who do you share meaningful insights with? Friends and family. This question and answer approach to relationship building puts you in the friends and family category for your client, separating you from other advisors who only care about *where* a client should invest.

A sales process is only as good as the questions asked. Good questions create great relationships. Good questions bridge means *and* meaning. They connect the client's means—what they have—with what they desire.

A sales process is only as good as the questions asked.

Clients are starved for a trusting professional who will ask authentic questions and really try to help them. They are tired of being asked questions based on a script and being led down a path only to be sold to at the end of it. Be real with your clients. Ask meaningful questions, and really try to get to know them.

Failing to ask meaningful questions can end in the wrong solution for the client. This creates buyer's remorse, kills the deal, and leaves the client without a real solution. Advisors who really understand the client weave the client's story into the solution. This not only helps the client, but it also sends a message that the advisor is listening and really cares.

Yes, it's important to get to know prospects and clients as people, but you also have to let them know you, too. So many advisors fail to realize clients don't just want an advisor; they want a personal relationship. They want to get to know you. You are more than just a financial advisor. Your unique story will connect clients to you.

Many elite advisors sell themselves by sharing their personal story before sharing product solutions. Alan watched Terry do this when they took appointments together. He saw that by opening up, the clients got to know Terry as a person, not just a financial professional. This two-sided connection creates a stronger bond than any professional connection, which strengthens client loyalty.

Chapter 14: Sell to Serve

Next time you go to make a sale, try the following:

1) Get to know the client on a personal level by asking detailed questions that unveil their relationship with money

2) Listen more than you talk

3) Weave the client's story into your solution

15

TELL GREAT STORIES

"We all have a life story and a message that can inspire others to live a better life or run a better business. Why not use that story and message to serve others and grow a real business doing it?"

— *Brendon Burchard*

No one buys products. They buy people. If you want a client to buy you, let them know you. Always connect on a personal level before presenting a solution.

Leave Your Prospects Hungry for More

You know my story. My passion for financial advising drove me to ask questions and learn as much as I could so I could ultimately help the advisors I spoke with. The real story, the one I wrote at the beginning of *Breakthrough*, differentiates me from other people who do what I do. You've got me idolizing my grandpa, looking to my dad for advice, and frantically learning as much as possible to succeed in a new business. Those details—the colors that bring a picture to life—are what make my story human. They are what make my story relatable.

If instead of adding color, I said, "I've been in this business for ten years, really enjoy what I do, and want to share some advice," you'd probably leave *Breakthrough* on the shelf. It's the human elements—my grandpa, my dad, my struggle—that tell the story and keep it interesting.

Make Yourself Unforgettable

I've attended hundreds of financial seminars throughout the last ten years. When it comes to storytelling and relating to an audience, I know what works well and what doesn't. I recognize techniques top advisors and great presenters use to make the ultimate impact with their audience.

Typically, advisors begin seminars by talking about their company. They talk about the business, not the people behind it. Then, they transition to charts, graphs, statistics, and financial jargon. It's fairly dry and impersonal. Honestly, it's often pretty obvious the audience is only half interested. I went to one seminar, however, that was not only unforgettable, but was also an incredible life lesson.

I was sitting in the back of the room when the advisor, Jean, was introduced. She walked to the front and started talking not about her company, but about herself. She started with her personal story. First, she talked about her childhood, sharing experiences that made her who she is today. She linked those formative experiences to the audience and her career, demonstrating to every client in the room why she chose her career and loved it so much.

In that five minutes it took for this advisor to tell her story, you could hear a pin drop. The audience was engaged and connected to Jean. I'd never seen anything like it before. It gave me chills.

I'd known Jean for a long time—I felt I knew her well—but after hearing that story, I connected with her on a much deeper level. Yes, I was sincerely interested in the financial information she covered, but I was empowered and entertained by her story. I discussed this with Jean in detail after the event, and discovered she actually had a few clients in the room as well as prospects. One of those clients later emailed Jean, thanked her for sharing her story, and said they felt they knew her better because of it.

Catapult Your Appointment-Setting Ratio

Another advisor, who similarly tweaked his seminar style, immediately increased his appointment-setting ratio from 55 percent to 70 percent. Sharing your story makes you a magnet for people's attention and loyalty. Why? Because clients don't buy a product. They buy a person.

Your story—who you are—is the connective tissue between you and your clients. It trumps any financial information you can offer. Don't be afraid to let people know who you are and what you stand for. This alone separates you from the other advisors out there. The more personal your story, the better the impact.

> Your story—who you are—is the connective tissue between you and your clients. It trumps any financial information you can offer.

Share your personal story, your emotions, and your motivations. Let clients know who you are. Add the touching, human details that paint a clear picture of you, this incredible *person* and advisor. Take every chance available to share your story. Let clients know how passionately you believe in what you're doing.

Become a Great Storyteller

Learn *how* to tell a story. Advisors who master the dramatic demonstration by successfully painting vivid pictures during a presentation have a much greater chance of engaging with—and developing relationships with—prospects.

Take clients through the twists and turns of your life. Show rather than tell exactly what made you the person you are today.

Use the power of the dramatic demonstration, which paints a vivid, long-lasting picture that connects to the audience emotionally; draw your audience in by creating a memorable scene.

Visual props such as charts and graphs can also help paint your story. For example, five years ago, we gave advisors a great chart that broke down the history of the stock market. The point of the chart was to help advisors with their sales processes. Many advisors used this tool with prospective clients to educate them about stock market history and how understanding that history will allow them to make better decisions today.

One of my top advisors said he found a way to use the chart to make a much bigger impact with clients. Instead of just showing the chart and pointing out this and that, this advisor memorized the chart. Like a teacher, he drew the chart on a white board at seminars dramatically demonstrating the turns of events. As he built momentum, clients wondered, "What's next?" This advisor converted the one-minute chart into a ten-minute discussion with clients who were more engaged as they felt the ups and downs in stock market history. This demonstration left them on the edge of their seats, which is something a standalone chart could never do.

Concepts that are shown engage the audience and connect to them in a way telling cannot. Shown stories stick in your client's memory. Imagine having a prospect think about the story you told later that evening during drinks with friends.

B O A R D

Chapter 15: Tell Great Stories

Showing your clients who you are by sharing a personal story will make them remember *and* trust you. Here's how to do it:

1) Stop leading your sales pitch with numbers and stats, and start leading with a personal story

2) Include emotional elements and your motivations in your story

3) Use the power of dramatic demonstration and props to add color to the stories you tell

16

BELIEVE IN WHAT YOU'RE SELLING

"I can sell anything that I totally
believe in, but I'm a horrible salesman
of something I don't believe in."
— *Nick Woodman*

A few years ago, one of my advisors had one of the worst years of his career, doing only around $4 million in new assets. The next year, his business exploded to more than $12 million, tripling his production.

When I see big production jumps, I'm always eager to ask the advisor what caused the breakthrough.

This advisor's response was so simple I couldn't believe it. He said, "I started believing in the products again."

Belief in what you sell and the difference you make for clients is crucial because the sale must be made in your head before it can be made with the client. To sell yourself on the sale, you have to believe the solution is right for the client. Once you have that belief, you will then transfer that belief to the client.

If you think about it, 90 percent of our communications are non-verbal. In fact, before we had well-developed language skills, almost all of our communications were nonverbal. If you *think* you're projecting your belief in a product, but you don't really *feel* that way, that disbelief will come through in your nonverbal actions. Without belief, you don't have a sale.

Consider this example. Imagine finding a product that costs $50 a month and having no option but to go to the client with an offer for the same product at a cost of $100 a month. You know the product that's twice as expensive provides the same solution as the cheaper option. This realization, of course, affects your ability to sell the product. Even if you're great salesperson, knowing you don't believe the $100 option is the best product for the client will affect your ability to make the sale. I've seen this with many advisors who are considered "captive," meaning they have to work for a company rather than the client. Captive advisors are typically restricted in terms of which products they can offer because their company must approve them. So, they can't shop the best rates or products, like independent advisors can.

Let's say a captive advisor works for company XYZ. XYZ has an annuity that the advisor must sell—it's their only choice. It offers the client $1,000 a month in income for a $100,000 premium. Because the advisor is captive, they must make that one annuity fit, or not make the sale at all. However, if they are independent like the advisors I work with, they can shop the market and possibly find another company that will give the client $1,500 a month for the same premium. What a difference $500 more a month with the same premium can make for a client! If you knew you could get someone a benefit of $500 more per month for the rest of their life or 50 percent more income, how excited would you be to sell that product? A lot more excited, right? On the flip side, how hard would it be to sell the inferior or more expensive product knowing they could get something better elsewhere?

Your Energy is Irresistible

I've worked with a lot of captive advisors who switched and became independent advisors. The first day they're independent, they're infused with a new energy. They're like a kid in a candy shop—they can't wait to sell all of the options available to them. It's like the handcuffs or shackles have been torn off, and they are free to offer whatever they want and whatever they see is best for their clients. Oftentimes, that newfound energy and belief rocket fuels these advisors successes. They can't wait to talk to clients about the solutions they can offer.

Great salespeople believe in their product, but they also believe in themselves. In fact, because we all sell something similar, many salespeople sell clients on themselves, their firm, and their unique process instead of on the product alone.

Consider this example. A client comes to you with a handful of quotes and wants to know, "How does your product compare to others?" First, you have to know you can compete on product offerings, like we've mentioned. However, starting a product war turns your business into a commodity. Before you know it, price is all that matters. Play a different game. Don't compete on price or product alone. Share your expertise, your process for developing the best solutions, and the value you add to the client. Product is only a fraction of what a relationship with you offers. Of course, in the end, the client also gets a good solution, but your unique process determines that experience and can differentiate you from the competition even more.

Set Yourself Apart from Other Advisors

Clients can get products anywhere, but they can only get your process and your expertise from you. Top advisors use this to their advantage. They map out their process step by step so clients completely understand it and the benefits of working with them. They let clients know the first step is making sure they understand their process up front and how they are able to help their clients. They take a few steps back before jumping into solutions to make sure the client has a good understanding of what they can expect while working with them. By the time the client gets through the process, they are so blown away by the advisor's close attention to detail and the advisor's ability to help them, that the end product solution was only part of the story. They received so much more value than they expected.

MAP YOUR PROCESS

Step 1: Discovery meeting, discover what's most important to you, gain a thorough understanding that goes beyond money

Step 2: Full analysis, see if that lines up correctly with your goals. Include fee, stress test, and so on. Is everything congruent with your goals?

Step 3: If necessary, make potential recommendations

Step 4: Implement changes if necessary

> Clients can get products anywhere, but they can only get your process and your expertise from you.

Your process—how you do what you do—must be outlined in detail. Give it a name, and start using that name so clients will start asking specifically for that process. Imagine naming your process the Financial Blueprint and hearing prospects say, "I want a Financial Blueprint, please."

How much more valuable is that than a prospect's asking for a second opinion? They can get a second opinion from anybody, but they can only get your process—your Financial Blueprint—from you.

The majority of clients don't understand financial nuances. When they ask for the Financial Blueprint, explain it well so they know each step of your process up front. Clients should understand that your process is unique. Describe it in detail and show how it benefits them. This way they aren't confused through your process, thinking, "Where is this going?" while you are presenting. Map it out in a simple, easy-to-understand way. Remember, anyone can offer them products. That's not really the biggest differentiator for you, but of course, you also want to make sure the clients understand the products that are used to implement their solution at the end of your process and how they work. You don't want clients thinking that your process and the products are one in the same. All of this needs to be clearly communicated.

One of our top advisors literally lays out her process on a big-screen TV in the meeting room so clients know exactly what each step looks like. Then they go through the process together. Her clients don't wonder what's next or when the pressure sale will come. Clients don't question what the advisor expects from them, or what they can expect from her. The advisor communicates her entire process up front so expectations and objectives are clear to everyone. No one is left guessing.

Once you've named your process, use it in marketing materials, and address it by name during sales meetings. Shout it from the rooftops. This is now one of your greatest differentiators, and the better you sell your process, the more valuable it will be because it's unique to you. No one else can offer it.

Belief translates to any aspect of your business that you're selling. If you sell your process, you really have to believe your process is better than others are. If you sell how your team manages money or how comprehensive your plans are, you have to believe your team is incredible, or that your plans will make a real difference. When you have that belief, guess what? Your belief transfers to the clients.

Top advisors believe wholeheartedly in the value they bring. Some salespeople may have product-specific confidence, others are confident in the quality, and impact of their process. Regardless of which driver they choose, they sell what they believe in, which is a motivating factor for advisors and staff.

From Down and Out to Top Advisor

Once I worked with an associate advisor who was really struggling. His sales were down, he felt sluggish and uninspired, and he was starting to question whether he wanted to continue with his career. Then, out of nowhere, it started to click. He started writing more and more business, and within a couple months, he became one of my top advisors. As always, when a huge improvement like this is made, I asked, "What happened?"

He said, "I was too focused on following the perfect sales script, using the right words, and making sure the process was perfect. One day, I sat down with a couple clients and it occurred to me: What we do as a company is much better than the service prospects are currently getting. These prospects were being neglected and being sold things they didn't need. I realized we could really help them."

As soon as the associate advisor realized he could really help his clients, sales started pouring in. Everything he'd concentrated on before was meaningless. Once he understood he could make a difference, he did.

Advisors, associate advisors, and staff need to believe in the difference they make for clients. With that belief comes an ability to do a much better job. Many of our offices start off each week with a success story from the previous week highlighting something they did for a client. This reminds everyone why they do what they do, and keeps belief centric to the team.

Imagine what a difference this can make to someone who is tired or bored. Sharing true stories with staff about the impact your firm has on clients hoists them out of slumps and reconnects them to their own mission. Share these experiences weekly. Together, compare how your work is different to that of a competitor's. These frequent reminders boost everyone's confidence and energy, which in turn increases productivity.

B O A R D

Chapter 16: Believe in What You're Selling

Share your belief with clients by:

1) Preparing for your next appointment by answering the question, "If a client came to me with handful of quotes, what sets me apart from the other advisors?"

2) Mapping out and naming your process

3) Differentiating yourself from competitors by selling your unique process

17

PRACTICE VALUE-BASED SELLING

*"Try not to become a man of success,
but rather a man of value."*

— *Albert Einstein*

I really believe there are 100 points to every sale. If you get all 100 points, the sale is made. You may score points by filling the void in a prospect's plan, solving a specific issue, or being more trustworthy and likeable than their current advisor. If you can solve their problem and fill their needs, and they like and trust you, you get 100 points. But there is so much you can do to add value to them on top of that. And for everything else you can do for them, you will get extra credit points. It's icing on the cake. The more value you stack, the higher your score. Don't aim for 100 points. Aim for more points by adding tremendous value to the client.

Think about it this way. Say you offer a client the best plan for their needs, which is the client's primary motive. However, as you get to know this client, you discover you can help with other things. You can provide better service and monthly education, neither of which is provided by their other advisor. Let's say with the help of your office or other industry experts, you can offer them assistance with taxes and estate-planning needs. This extra credit gives you 120 points instead of 100. With that score, you've seriously exceeded expectations. You've gone above and beyond. The decision between staying with their existing advisor and switching to you is a no brainer: you've got the job.

The One Question That Can Close Almost Any Sale

If you want to add clients, the question is always, "How can I add more and more value to every single client?"

I was at an event a few years back and, with the event speaker, I was talking to an advisor who said, "I don't feel I'm doing a good job selling my prospects. How can I improve?"

The speaker said, "You're asking the wrong question."

The question isn't, "How do you get better at sales? It's how do you add more value?" More than likely, in this example, the advisor was not adding enough value, decreasing the chance of a sale. So many people look at sales as the art of talking to a client or giving a presentation when it's really about value. How can you become more valuable? What else can you offer? What else can you do for your clients?

Value Trumps Sales Skills

If you find ways to add more and more value to the prospect, sales becomes much easier.

Think about it this way. Let's say we have two different advisors. One is a great sales person. He says everything correctly, he's well-polished, and he has a killer sales presentation. However, he doesn't have any support, resources, or added benefits beyond financial solutions. He is a one-man show. The clients who have him have only him.

The second advisor is an okay salesperson. He's less polished, works for a company that has fifteen employees, a legal team, tax team, and multiple systems for adding value to clients. They meet clients quarterly, host educational events, and add a ton of value outside of finance. When clients have this advisor, they have an entire team committed to adding an unprecedented amount of value outside of financial services.

> # Don't add 10 percent more value than your competition. Add ten times more value than your competition.

Although advisor one is a better sales person, advisor two offers so much more value that there's less pressure on him to sell. The sales are easier. Advisor two wins.

Captivate More Market Share from Day One

Consider this. Advisors Excel has an advisor who has such a great team that his new advisors become hugely successful within the first year of working for him. It isn't that this advisor picks the right advisors to work for him, it's that his business—his systems —are set up so well that they are less dependent on the sales ability of the advisors than most practices. They offer so much value, sales come more easily, and everyone enjoys more success.

One of my top advisors recently echoed this idea. He said the key to success in sales is stacking value.

Value begins with the first touchpoint between your firm and the client and continues throughout the relationship. Every single interaction is an opportunity to add value.

When you wake up in the morning, your first thought should be, "How can I add value to my clients today?"

Don't add 10 percent more value than your competition. Add ten times more value than your competition. Your top client is your competition's top prospect. With more than 300,000 choices out there, it's a buyer's market. The last thing you want is a client jumping to a competitor because of something you didn't offer. When you add value, your business becomes more valuable. The more valuable you are, the more market share you capture.

True value creates real value outside the products and services offered. You've got to find out what your clients want and what they think they want. Get to know clients on a personal level and understand their motivations so you can develop a deep relationship with them quickly. What's in their head? What concerns can you help with? Can you find a way to help them with those issues? Find answers to these questions and you will become more valuable.

One of my top advisors heard his clients wanted someone to integrate their taxes, estate planning, and finances. They felt nothing was connected—the tax guy did this, the finance guy this, the estate planning guy that. So what did my advisor do? He built systems and a qualified, licensed team within his office to integrate all three. Together, they coordinated financial, legal, and tax matters in one harmonious plan. The documents are packaged in one professional, organized binder, and given to clients with an updated balance sheet based on portfolio returns from year to year.

You don't have to hire an estate planning attorney, or a certified public accountant (CPA). You can, of course, but you can also be the connector—the go-to guy or girl for these resources. Build a relationship with a CPA and attorney and have them come to the office once a week to help clients. You are the connector, the value comes from you.

Think about it this way. Say a girl bypasses her boyfriend for homework help and goes to a guy friend instead. Her reason? The friend is better at math. The girlfriend goes to a competitor because the competitor offers something the boyfriend doesn't. You don't want your clients talking to a competitor about anything if you can provide it for them, either through in-house staff or external industry experts. Not consolidating financial information, not investment objectives, not decreasing taxes. Nothing. Adding value means becoming the go-to guy or gal for your clients. Find the problem and then add value.

There are a lot of little, easy, ways you can add more and more value to your clients. Maybe you offer a beneficiary review to ensure a client's beneficiary designations are in order, correct, and up-to-date. Maybe you offer a complete retirement income analysis showing the client exactly how their retirement income needs are met as well as what they might want to watch for. Constantly ask about the needs and wants of clients and prospects. Do this and not only will your current clients be happier, your sales process will become easier.

I have a client who hosts an educational event for current clients every two weeks. His clients are hungry for knowledge. They want to learn about their investments. Guess what? Now when this advisor sits down with prospects, because he knows existing clients like education, he knows his prospects probably will, too. He lets prospects know about the educational sessions and suggests they attend the next one. He also asks prospects if they're used to that type of education. They always say no. Their current advisors don't do anything like that. In fact, they only see their current advisor once a year. This advisor, on the other hand, constantly sees and educates them. This is an unfair advantage. This is what happens. The prospect goes in for help with their retirement plan but leaves thinking about how great it would be to have access to educational topics their current advisor doesn't offer. More and more unexpected value equals lots of extra credit points.

Remember, at the end of the day, he or she who brings the most value wins.

Remember, at the end of the day, he or she who brings the most value wins.

I once heard a story that Michael Jordan used to take referees to dinner. This allowed him to build great relationships with the referees, which naturally had an impact on the court. The other players had no idea what game Jordan was really playing. They were competing on the court, but Jordan was playing a whole separate game off of it. Ask yourself how you can play a bigger game than your competition, one they don't even know is happening. What can you do to offer more and more value to clients and prospects?

Add So Much Value Clients Feel *Compelled* to do Business with You

Realize this business is a lot bigger than the products. Every advisor sells some version of the same product. It may be a small differentiator at times, but the biggest differentiator has nothing to do with product. Of course, you will always want to offer the best deal, understand the products inside and out, and know the key features and benefits. But what can you do on top of that to offer value?

Imagine if clients had to subscribe to your services for a monthly fee. Do you add enough value that your clients would write a check every month for your ongoing services? If not, what can you create to add value so they would pay that fee? Embark on a quest to discover what your clients value and what your office can offer to fulfill that need. Figure out what they'd pay a small monthly fee for and what they'd pay a premium price for, but don't charge them. Win their loyalty. It's worth much more than any amount of money you could gain.

If there's 100 points to every sale, good advisors score 100. Great advisors score 120. Not only do they listen to clients, they provide the best solutions and, most importantly, build tremendous value.

One advisor told me Advisors Excel offered so much value, he felt guilty every time we sent him anything. Our service was above and beyond what he expected, which was such an incredible experience, he had to do business with us. This is the beauty of the law of reciprocity. Bring so much value to your clients that they have to do business with you.

Those who add value forget about *wanting* and focus on *giving*. Giving is the only way to establish a real, lasting connection. Focusing solely on what you can get out of a relationship is the fastest way to developing meaningless connections. The law of reciprocity says the more you give, the more you receive. In this business, it's no different.

Chapter 17: Practice Value-Based Selling

The advisor who adds the most value wins.

1) Do you add enough value that your clients would write a check every month for your ongoing services?

2) How can you add more value to your clients so they would actually be willing to pay a premium for your services?

3) Listen to your clients on an ongoing basis and start building systems within your business to be more valuable

18

ADOPT THESE SIX STEPS TO BULLETPROOF THE SALE

"It's not about having the right opportunities,
it's about handling the opportunities right."
— *Mark Hunter*

After observing what hundreds of the best advisors say, how they say it, and how they develop their processes, I've found the best of the best follow set sales structures during every single meeting. They do not fly by the seat of their pants. They do not reinvent themselves or their process during each meeting. They find a familiar format and use it for every appointment.

A while back, I had a young advisor, Mark, whom I considered a sales genius. At 27 years old, Mark brought in more production with clients who were twice his age than advisors who were twice his age did. Mark didn't have gray hair and experience, so people didn't automatically trust him. He had to pay close attention to every detail of his process and do everything he could to overcompensate for what he lacked by making sure his process was as impactful as possible. He did it by developing—and sticking to—this six-step process for every sale.

1. Build rapport
2. Identify the problem
3. Get the client to agree with the problem
4. Agree on a solution
5. Validate the solution
6. Bulletproof the sale

Every advisor has a different process and structure, but Mark found his chances of closing a sale increased dramatically whenever he successfully completed all six of these steps. These steps may seem simple, but there's more to them than meets the eye.

Step 1: Build Rapport

The first step—establishing professional rapport with the *correct* expectations—sets the groundwork for developing a good relationship with the prospect. Rapport is all about getting the prospect to like you, trust you, and realize you're capable of meeting their needs.

We have talked about sharing your story and really getting to know the client, which is part of this step. This step also includes letting the prospect know your process and expectations up front so they take your time seriously. This lets the prospect know what you expect from them, as well as what they can expect from you. Both of you can do your part and the relationship is built on mutual respect.

If a prospect doesn't like or trust you, they won't become a client. If they come in but won't share any information, they don't trust you. If they think they're in control of the meeting and you're just an order taker, they don't understand expectations. In these situations, nothing you say or do will get the sale. However, you probably don't want the sale anyway because the prospect is likely not a good fit.

Everything you do before meeting the prospect enhances or diminishes your rapport with them. If you've dressed to impress, your team has been spot on in their interactions with the prospect, and your office impresses, the rapport process will be easy and minimal. However, if you arrive late in jeans and a t-shirt, the staff forgot to return the client's call, or spoke unprofessionally to them, and the office is a dump, building rapport will be an uphill battle.

For a productive meeting to take place, the client must be comfortable. Verbal and non-verbal communication plays a role here. Speaking confidently, using strong rather than weak language, listening, and practicing patience all affect rapport. Every action should reflect how much you care about that prospect. Establishing that up front with the prospect is your main priority. Maintain control of the meeting by setting expectations for the process and the relationship and set these early and clearly. You've chosen to be with the prospect, just as they've chosen to be with you. It's a mutually beneficial relationship.

Step 2: Identify the Problem

When the prospect is comfortable and rapport has been established, the next step is to identify the need or problem. As we have discussed before, ask good questions, be authentic, and empathetically identify their real need.

Do not lead the prospect down a path of a certain solution or toward a problem they do not have just because you want a sale. The problem must be a real problem for the prospect, not a problem you hope they have so you can get a sale. For example, don't tell a prospect who isn't concerned about running out of money that they may run out of money and offer a solution that fixes that problem. One of my top advisors said misdiagnosing the problem is one of the biggest mistakes salespeople make. They see an issue—or perceived issue— for the prospect, and don't dig deeper to make sure the issue is real to the prospect.

Dig in, ask more questions, and get a clear understanding of your prospect's concerns. So many people pounce as soon as they get a whiff of an issue they can fix. The better you understand what the prospect needs, the more likely you are to help them. Actively listen to what the prospect says, show genuine concern, and speak without an agenda.

Step 3: Get the Client to Agree with the Problem

Once you understand the prospect's needs, practice active listening. Mark, the young advisor who shared these steps, repeats the prospect's concerns back to them in his own words—to make sure he is on track—and asks them to confirm that what he said is correct. He shows he's really listening and has the prospect agree that he understands the situation before they move on.

Once you know the problem, decide if it's big enough to act on. So many people will agree the problem exists, but it isn't big enough to do anything about. If the prospect doesn't agree the problem is big enough to fix, there's no use offering a solution. I have some advisors who actually have the prospect say—or write down—that they want to fix the problem. They get the prospect to take ownership of the problem by agreeing to fix it. If the prospect doesn't understand how big the problem is or doesn't believe it needs to be fixed, no sale will be made.

Step 4: Agree on a Solution

Once the prospect agrees there's a problem and that they want to fix it, introduce the solution. The solution—what you're selling—can be a number of things including a product, you, your company, or your process. The best salespeople have a gift for simplifying complex things. This is where that gift pays off. No matter how complex the solution, make it easy for the prospect to understand. Jumping into details and minutia prematurely will cause confusion and get you in trouble. Spewing technical jargon before the prospect understands the solution will overwhelm and paralyze them. They won't buy.

The best salespeople have a gift
for simplifying complex things.

Once the prospect understands the concept of the solution at a high level, check in and see whether the prospect agrees the potential solution will work for them. Once they agree, move to the next step, which is validating the solution.

Step 5: Validate the Solution

To validate the solution, provide details and specifics that show what the prospect wanted is real. You can also validate the solution by sharing any research or evidence that supports your claims. Answer every question, whether it's between the prospect and their spouse, or addressed directly to you. The last thing you want is the prospect leaving the office with unanswered questions.

Throughout this process, you and the prospect agree over and over again about what needs to be done. Selling is nothing more than a series of agreements between you and your prospect. Eventually, the little agreements add up to one big agreement. That is, the prospect agrees to work with you because you've agreed to fulfill their conditions of satisfaction.

> Selling is nothing more than a series of agreements between you and your prospect.

At the point of validation, the sale is made, right? We have a yes, so it's time to celebrate, right? Not so fast. Far too many advisors leave appointments and celebrate a "new client" before the sale is over. Unfortunately, just because the prospect agreed to work with you at the time, doesn't mean they will. The hardest part of the process is the conversation the client will have with their current advisor.

Step 6: Bulletproof the Sale

The last step in the process is bulletproofing the sale, or seal-ing the deal. The prospect says yes, I'm in. Now it's time for you to coach the prospect through the process and let them know exactly what to expect next. Oftentimes the start of a new rela-tionship means the end of another, so we may need to address the exit, or divorce, from that other advisor. This will prevent surprises later on. If by chance they don't have another advi-sor, you still need to share expectations and timelines so they know what's coming.

How to Keep New Clients from Backing Out

Many clients feel they owe it to the other advisor to tell them what they're doing and why they're moving on. Some do this on the phone. Others do it in person. Either way, the sale is not final until the client has finished their relationship with the incumbent advisor. Bulletproofing the sale prepares clients to meet incum-bent advisors and coaches them on the exit so there's nothing the existing advisor can do or say to change that prospect's mind. Cli-ents who are not coached are much more likely to be talked out of making the change.

When given the opportunity, an incumbent advisor will often try to talk your new client out of working with you. They may try to show them problems with your solutions, or may discuss how they are better equipped to help them than you are. Either way, they will suggest making the change is a huge mistake, which in turn could lead the valued client to fall off your radar. A simple discussion at the end of your sales process can generally prepare the client for this conversation and keep this from happening. This is another area you can better prepare them for. It also gives you an opportunity to shine by making things easier on the client.

At the end of the meeting, if your prospect plans to meet with their advisor, let the prospect know the easy part is over, and that it's sometimes tough to have that conversation with the former advisor. They'll agree. Ask them if they have good rapport with the other advisor. They will say something along the lines of, "Yes, we've been with him for years."

Respond by saying, "Okay good. It's not easy, but more than likely they'll respect your decision in the end."

Then say something to you client like, "We can make this process as easy or as hard as we want to. With your permission, I'd like to share what I've learned from others to make it a little easier on you."

They'll agree.

Then let the client know that in your experience, when clients let their former advisor know they're changing advisors, the advisor typically wants some feedback as to why the client is making the change. Let your client know to feel free to share whatever they are comfortable sharing with their advisor about the change. However, be sure to let the client know upfront that typically the first time they mention the change to their current advisor, the advisor will likely try and talk them out of it. However, once they say a second time that their decision is final, the advisor will usually respect that decision.

One advisor I work with even lets his clients know the common objections the incumbent advisor will raise when clients talk to them about changing advisors. For example, this advisor will explain that typically the current advisor will have only one of two responses when the client lets them know that they are ready to make the change. The incumbent advisor will either say, "this is bad altogether" and try to tell them the plan or change is wrong. Or, they may respond by saying, "I can do this, too" as if the new direction is something the incumbent can handle so the client doesn't have to make a change. In the end, the clients realize with both of these two declarations, the real intent of the advisor is to keep the business.

My advisor will then go as far as telling his clients, "This isn't the advisor's money, it's not my money, it's your money, right?"

The clients of course say, "yes."

He'll then let them know that they are right and in that case all that really matters is how they feel about it and they obviously feel that this change is what's best for them.

The interesting thing is that when the new advisor discusses these common objections, the client is totally prepared for the conversation with the incumbent advisor. This mitigates the incumbent advisor's sales tactic, so in the end, clients are much more likely to stay the course in taking the corrective action they felt was right after meeting with my advisor.

If you do this, you will have prepared your client so well for that conversation that they can accomplish what they were hoping for in such a way that they are not caught off guard.

Another key element to bulletproofing the sale is what you do after the sale. Just because the sale is over, doesn't mean you should stop talking to your prospect. In fact, that's when you should throw open the lines of communication for the days to come.

Once the client signs on the dotted line, reconfirm with every step of your process that they made the right decision. Don't let the client fall off your radar just because they've said yes.

Stop Buyer's Remorse in Its Tracks

Most advisors send a thank-you note to a new client. They might even include a Starbucks gift card. The feeling the client gets from a couple of free cups of coffee will last a couple of days, maybe even a week. Why not give the client something that will stay in front of them long-term?

The first sixty days of a relationship are the most critical to building that relationship. I know an advisor who uses those sixty days to provide as much value as he can to his new clients. Basically, immediately after the sale, he sends high-quality, valuable letters and communications to clients that are full of useful updates. These include multiple touchpoints made throughout the first weeks of the relationship starting with a high-end kit welcoming them to the family. The package includes a company branded cozy blanket, heavy drinks glasses, coasters, playing cards, and many other items. This kit ensures every new relationship starts with a thank-you. Oddly enough, that thank-you doesn't come from the advisor. It comes from client. Clients always call my advisor's office to thank them for the nice gift. The client makes the contact.

Following the welcome package, my advisor has a key team member send a handwritten thank-you note to the client. It includes a personal comment from a staff member who is looking forward to talking with and meeting the new client as well as an invitation for the client to call anytime they need something. They also send a letter that explains my advisor's team approach, adding that each member of the team is excited to meet and work with the client. Information about key members of the team, their roles within the company, and their photos are also included. This approach establishes that going forward, the relationships will involve the team, not just the advisor. An additional letter invites the client to join one of many training events hosted by my advisor's team.

Again, the law of reciprocity applies here. Give, give, give. People are not used to this level of giving from their advisor. Giving blows buyer's remorse out of the water.

This series of touches following a yes reduces the likelihood of buyer's remorse, stops misconceptions, and ensures questions get answered immediately.

While sales processes vary from advisor to advisor, these six basic steps provide a solid guideline for every advisor. A sales process is particularly critical for new advisors, but as your credibility increases, the pressure on each step of the sales process will decrease.

Chapter 18: Adopt These Six Steps to Bulletproof the Sale

Nail your sales process by:

1) Setting the right expectations with clients up front

2) Having your client take ownership of the problem

3) Keeping yourself at the forefront of your client's mind after the sale by sending them a series of high-quality communications during your first sixty days together

19

OBJECTIONS MADE EASY

"Objections are only questions or concerns
that you have failed to address."

— *Elite Advisor, AZ*

Regardless of how effective your sales process is, you will have to address questions, concerns, and objections from clients. Whether those objections affect your end result is entirely up to you

Head Objections off at the Pass

Some objections may stop you in your tracks; others may go so well they don't feel like objections at all. One of the advisors at Advisors Excel shared an unforgettable lesson. He said, "The objections you get are just the result of your faulty sales process."

He wasn't implying that advisors don't get objections, or tough questions. He was implying that the size and type of objections you'll receive are completely within your control.

Tough objections are usually prompted by something in your sales process, so the first step in refuting objections is identifying which objections are most common in your process. So many advisors face the same objections over and over and never ask, "How can I get rid of this objection so it's no longer an obstacle? What is the best way to handle this? What can I do so this no longer comes up?

Ask yourself: What are the three most common objections I get?

If you don't know the answer, you're not improving like you should. Figure out the answer, and stop those dreaded objections by learning the best way to handle them.

If you see enough people, common objections become crystal clear. Common objections often unveil critical information that's skipped over and missed during a presentation, or—more importantly—what needs to be discussed in more detail during the presentation.

Let's say you struggle with the objection, "How safe is my money with this product or insurance company?"

Imagine giving a one-hour presentation on the level of protection associated with that product or company. For one hundred percent of the presentation, that's the topic. Do you think anyone would raise their hand at the end of that meeting and ask, "How safe is my money with this product or insurance company?" No, because you've covered it so thoroughly.

Obviously, the strength of an insurance product is that it's backed by the carrier and there are different ways to evaluate each carrier. Talk to the client about this in detail so they won't surprise you with a question at the end of your meeting.

Override Remaining Objections Smoothly and Painlessly

The level of safety and risk associated with a product is critical to a client's buying decision. Wouldn't it make sense to address those concerns up front? If you're getting the question, you're not addressing the concern enough.

If an objection arises at the end of a meeting, react in a way that has proven to fulfill the client's needs and positions you for success. As with your sales process, be prepared. Have a proven, well-thought-out method for handling these objections so that it's simple and easy for them to understand.

As with your sales process, be prepared. Have a proven, well-thought-out method for handling these objections so that it's simple and easy for them to understand.

Objections show what matter to clients. Assess each, find the solution, and work it into your presentation or appointment. Once the objections have been identified, be the first to take them off the table.

I asked one of my favorite advisors how he handles the common objection, "It sounds too good to be true."

He rattled off some answers, but it seemed like if the question came from a client, he would backpedal, say whatever came to mind, and hope for the best. It wasn't a set, structured, proven response. He isn't alone. Numerous advisors don't have a proven way to respond to the most common objections.

One of my other advisors said the objection "it sounds too good to be true" will typically come up when the advisor hasn't clearly explained the solution to the client. This advisor said that if an advisor puts a lot of emphasis on the features and benefits that a solution offers without a thorough overview of the costs and restrictions, it may seem too good to be true. Your duty as an advisor is to make sure they have a well-rounded overview of the costs, restrictions, benefits, and features. If you do this, the objection won't come up.

I'm not suggesting the advisor who doesn't talk about all of the benefits and restrictions is withholding critical information intentionally, either. They may just be emphasizing the highlights in a way that seems almost oversold or unrealistic. By leveling the process out, you more than likely won't get this objection.

The advisor who shared the above advice went on to say he actually uses the dreaded words "it sounds too good to be true" in his own presentations to clients because when he first learned about the solutions, he thought they might be too good to be true. However, once he did his full due diligence, that wasn't necessarily the case.

In that instance, this advisor might say to a client: "Mr. Jones, I have to be honest with you here. I have tons of experience in every aspect of investments, insurance, and financial products. When I first saw this, I thought it was too good to be true. However, when I dug into the details and realized how it worked, I found the benefits would fit your particular need well."

Because he actually uses those words, he pretty much takes the objection off of the table.

Can you imagine a client coming back with "it sounds too good to be true" after you say that? Once you remove the objection, you literally take the words right out of the client's mouth. I suggested that one of my favorite advisors—the one who backpedaled when I originally raised the objection—try this other advisor's approach. The result was fantastic. Once he tried this, his clients no longer raised the objection. So how can you answer your most common objections and take them off the table for good?

> Once you remove the objection,
> you literally take the words right
> out of the client's mouth.

You first have to be aware of the objections that you are getting and think through what you can do to better inform the client on the front end. Is there a way you can address the objection before the client brings it up? Can you implant answers to the objection in your process? If you don't feel you are missing key information, the next best thing is to learn to react to the objection in a way that works well for the client and gives them a better understanding. Once you know how to handle an objection, you'll be comfortable and confident when it comes up.

The Perfect Script for Overcoming "I Need to Think About It"

One advisor I work with, Paul, is great at handling objections because he pays close attention to every detail of his sales process. His goal is to make the biggest impact he can with the people he's sitting down with.

There was an occasion in particular that I witnessed where Paul just blew my mind. Paul asked me if I'd like to sit in his appointment with a prospective client and observe. I was thrilled by the opportunity to learn from him and see his process first-hand.

I was at his office in a rather large conference room when the prospective clients came in and sat down. This was not the first meeting with these prospects. In fact, they'd had a couple meetings already. When Paul got to the point in the process where it was time to present the details of his plan to the prospects, I remember being nervous and trying not to make a sound just like a fly on the wall.

The presentation went great. The couple seemed very happy with what Paul showed them, and everybody seemed to be on the same page. Finally, towards the end of the meeting, there was a lull in the conversation. We were at the end and a decision needed to be made. Without moving, without even blinking, the woman took one look at her husband and said, "We need to think about it."

He muttered, "Uh huh."

He didn't even open his mouth.

They ESPed an inscrutable objection to each other. Now if you've ever gotten that objection at the end of a meeting, you understand it typically leads to a no, which is what I expected after hearing the dreaded words. The funny thing was, I really thought they were interested and happy with the solutions that Paul provided. I was definitely surprised as I thought it was final—no deal—but that's when Paul turned to the whiteboard as if none of this phased him at all.

This was routine for Paul. He'd been here before. I was wide-eyed and afraid to make a sound. Paul calmly pointed at the drawing on the whiteboard where he had presented his plan, shook his head and said, "You know, there is a lot of information up here. I can imagine this is overwhelming for you two today."

Paul paused. The couple shook their head in agreement and said, "It really is, Paul."

"You know, I've found this to be the case with a lot of my clients the first time we discuss this," Paul said. "There's a lot to it, but what I've found with most clients, is that it's best to make one decision at a time. Think about it. When you first decided to meet with me, your current portfolio had a problem. It didn't line up with your retirement goals. Is that right?"

The couple nodded their heads yes.

"Well, we both agree it's a problem, and we've discussed how big of a problem it really is," Paul said. "I believe it's a problem that needs to be fixed, but all that matters is what you believe. Do you feel like it's something you should fix?"

The wife nodded. The husband said, "Yes, it's a huge problem for us, which is why we came to you. We need this fixed."

"Okay," Paul said. For the first time in ten minutes, I relaxed my shoulders.

Paul continued. "The thing we need to figure out today, is who you feel is in the best position to help you. Your current relationship put you in this situation in the first place. Is that the relationship that is best able to help you?"

"No," the husband said.

"Okay. Forget all of this financial jargon for a minute," Paul waved at the whiteboard. "I don't want that to overwhelm you. You've already mentioned you aren't interested in working with your current advisor, and you don't feel they are best to fulfill your needs. As you have seen, we are very thorough in what we do and we are committed to working with you and helping you going forward. Today, all I'd really like to know from you, is will you hire me and my team to help you?

The couple looked at each other, nodded their heads, and said, "Yes, we think you are the best person to help us. We don't want to have to worry about this anymore."

They shook hands, smiled, and agreed to do business together. Paul asked a licensed associate to take care of the paperwork and he and I headed to lunch.

Clearly this was not the first time Paul heard this objection. It didn't give him any trouble at all. He knew what was best for the clients, but realized they had too much to think about and were too overwhelmed to make a decision. For a minute, they were in a paralyzed state. Paul knew the best approach was to simplify things so the couple could make a decision. He handled the situation like a pro and got the business. More importantly, the clients left his office that day in a better place than when they arrived. The majority of advisors would have ended the meeting hoping to meet with the clients again, and the clients very easily could have left with the same problems and concerns that they arrived with.

Paul's story demonstrates how paying attention to detail, and learning from objections gives advisors an advantage during the sales process. So many advisors hear an objection and move on without contemplating the best way to handle the objection. Paul thought about his common objections and responded to them proactively by breaking down the big decision into four little ones. As we said before, sales is really a series of agreements. In this instance, Paul and the client agreed numerous times throughout the meeting but in the end, four little agreements led to one big one.

At lunch, Paul said he used to dread objections, but once he learned to handle them, he started looking forward to them because he knew how to handle them. I know it's hard to believe, but learn the root cause of objections, learn the right way to approach them, and you'll start looking forward to them, too. Often times, clients don't intend their objections as a firm no. They're really just overwhelmed and need the decision simplified.

Often times, clients don't intend
their objections as a firm no.
They're really just overwhelmed
and need the decision simplified.

We all have to learn to overcome objections. Like many of you, I started my career cold calling hundreds of people a day, people who were not only not expecting the call, but were used to getting calls from people like me every day. These people were adverse to the call and programmed to just get off the phone as fast as they could because they saw no value in the conversation.

When I first started, a tough objection would stop me in my tracks. Then, once I heard it, I would go research ways to get over it. Within months, I found that 90 percent of the objections I was getting on a cold call could go into four main categories: Not interested; too busy, can't talk now; send me information; I'm already taken care of.

While they didn't use the same words every time, their objections fell into these categories. The deeper meaning was the same. Some would say, "I'm too busy and can't talk now," others would say, "You caught me at a bad time, call me later." Same meaning, different words.

Because I was aware of what the objections were, I found a way to overcome them through research and started putting my strategies into practice. When someone said "I am too busy," for example, I'd say "I totally understand. The only reason I was calling is (XYZ EXCITING THING)." Basically, if I finished the sentence with something that was exciting and attractive to them, they'd continue the call. If not, we'd hang up. Very rarely were they really too busy. It was just an excuse to get me off the phone.

Once I anticipated the objections, I would look forward to overcoming them. Suddenly, I was on the phone with prospects who were too busy to talk having a great conversation thirty minutes later. This progression starts with being aware of the objections and then finding a way to overcome them or minimize their damage.

Take a look at your top objections, find ways to implant answers to them in your sales process, and find the best ways to handle them. Sometimes during the sales process, we have to nudge our clients along. Sometimes objections are not a reason *not* to do business, but a statement—or question—designed to break down the complexity of the decision. Simplification makes all the difference in the world.

B O A R D

Chapter 19: Objections Made Easy

Don't let objections control you. Ask yourself:

1) What objections are most common in my sales process?

2) How can I address these objections during my sales process before they're raised?

3) How can I pay better attention to clients during my sales process to understand the motivations behind their objections?

20

SEAL THE DEAL LIKE A PRO

"Timid salesmen have skinny kids."
— *Zig Ziglar*

O ne of my top advisors recently said the one thing that separates good advisors from bad ones, is that good advisors are not afraid to ask for the business. As silly as it sounds, a lot of new salespeople don't ask for the business so guess what? They don't get it.

It doesn't matter how good your presentation is, if you don't ask for the business you won't get it. Believe in what you are selling, be confident that you're providing the best solution for the prospect, and then ask for the business. Always assume the prospect wants to do business with you.

This approach does not mean you should have a high-pressure sales process. Think of it this way. The prospect has a problem and you know what it would take to fix the problem and put them in a better position. But for them to be in a better place, they've got to take corrective action and that involves working with you. So many advisors either give prospects too many choices, which is confusing, or are too afraid to ask for the order. In either case, the sale walks out the door. Be willing to say, "This is the answer," and then assume the prospect will want to make your recommended changes. Your ability to do this makes all the difference in the world to the prospect. Besides, after all the great questions you've asked them, you should have a great understanding by now of who they are and how you can help them.

Get Clients to Ask YOU for the Sale

One of my top advisors is so good at closing he actually gets his clients to ask for the sale. By the time he finishes his presentation, the prospect shows a high level of interest, both he and the prospect have agreed multiple times that they're headed in the right direction, and he doesn't ask the prospect to buy. He gives the prospect a chance to move forward on their own by ending the meeting with this question: "Okay, you've seen what I have for you. Do you have any questions for me?"

My advisor has added so much value and the clients are so confident and comfortable that he can help them that they almost always respond with one of three questions: "What's the next step?" "Where do we go from here?" "How do we move forward?"

As opposed to the advisor asking the client to buy, the client asks the advisor to do business.

This advisor then asks for a copy of their driver's license, or suggests they move forward with paperwork. That's it. The prospect asks for the sale, so my advisor doesn't have to close. The advisor makes it easy for the prospect and therefore doesn't have to intensify the sales pressure.

If the prospect doesn't ask about the next steps or moving forward and instead says, "No, I don't really have any questions," or, "I can't think of any questions," the advisor asks if they're sure. Is there anything they can think of? This is a second shot at the same response. More often than not, prospects close themselves. Again, if you haven't spent the time getting to know their real issues and understand how you can help them, if you haven't added tremendous value to them up to this point, it probably won't work for you.

If the first two tries don't work, my advisor will then make the suggestion that they should do business together. He'll say something like, "It sounds like I've answered all of your questions here.

And, based on everything you've told me, this seems like a great fit. Do you agree?"

After they agree, he says, "Great! Let's get the paperwork taken care of. Do you have a copy of your driver's license?"

Make It Easy for Clients to Say "Yes"

Prospects want to buy, but some may want a professional who isn't afraid to help guide them in making decisions that are right for them. If you are unsure about what you're offering, the prospect will be, too. There's no reason to put any doubt in their mind. What you are doing is what you believe is right for them. You've got to be willing to tell them that and make it easy on them to implement the changes.

No matter how good your process is, never forget to ask for the business.

No matter how good your process is, never forget to ask for the business.

BOARD

Chapter 20: Seal the Deal Like a Pro

Never forget to ask for the business. Here are three key factors in sealing the deal:

1. Be sincerely convinced your prospects need your help

2. Don't be afraid to ask for the business

3. Do so well that the clients ask you for the business

21

SET REALISTIC EXPECTATIONS

"Exceed your customer's expectations. If you do, they'll come back over and over. Give them what they want—and a little more."

— *Sam Walton*

You know what it takes to get a sale. You understand the importance of believing in what you're selling, asking great questions, and getting clients to know you on a personal level. Each of these components are critical to sales. However, you've also got to be sure what you're selling is realistic for the client and that your promise is attainable. Otherwise, in time you may wish you didn't make the sale at all.

Create Long-Term Happiness for Yourself *and* Your Client

The key isn't to *just* get a sale, it's to get a sale while also setting the correct expectations. How well you set expectations determines the long-term satisfaction of your clients as well as the potential of your business.

Appropriate, realistic expectations must be set from the start or both you and the client will suffer. For example, an advisor who sells a product or investment based on its highest potential growth sets an unrealistic expectation. That growth is not a foregone conclusion. Even if the product performs well, the client will be upset because they expected more. If the advisor sets a proper expectation—a realistic expectation—the client will be thrilled when results exceed that expectation.

Failure to set realistic expectations can lead to short-term success—a new client, perhaps—but make long-term relationships impossible. Let's say the product does well in year one. What about year two or three? Even if the advisor makes good during the first year, their relationship with the client is on pins and needles from year to year because the original expectation was unrealistic. Also, trying to predict or over-promise product performance is a surefire way to increase your regulatory risk, since market performance is something that is outside of your control.

How Realism Wins Business

Advisors often set unrealistic expectations when they desperately need a sale. I've seen several newer advisors who genuinely felt they needed to promise the world in order to seal the deal. One advisor reminded me of this point when he shared this story. He had a client who shopped several advisors for a specific investment. With all the competition, my advisor knew better than to overpromise. He really wanted to show the client what was realistic, and he hoped that by doing so, he'd win the business. Rather than exaggerate, or inflate returns, my advisor set correct expectations. He also made sure the client understood the product's pros and cons. It's always better to share pros and cons immediately. Again, clients hate surprises.

Although my advisor knew the client was shopping around, he didn't change his process and did everything correctly from the beginning. In the end, the client hired my advisor. My advisor asked the client why he chose him. The client said that he was the only advisor who, in addition to talking about the product's advantages, also addressed its disadvantages. Every other advisor shared promises of past index returns without sharing the strings attached. Because my advisor shared both, the client trusted him more than he did the other advisors. The advisor was realistic. He didn't set expectations based on pie-in-the-sky returns so he got the business. Never base expectations on things you can't control. This leaves the relationship vulnerable to an uncertain outcome.

> # Never base expectations on things you can't control. This leaves the relationship vulnerable to an uncertain outcome.

Setting realistic expectations is not just about the product or solution you offer. It's about setting correct expectations with the client regarding your company and the service you provide as well. Communicate with clients immediately about how your business functions. Make sure they understand how your business operates and deliver the level of service promised.

The Horrifying Consequences of Overpromising

One of Advisor Excel's top producers said advisors who want the sale bad enough often pay too high a price for it. These advisors stretch promises to get the business. They may overpromise personal service or expected returns. It never turns out well.

Consider this horror story. A few years ago, a top advisor, who was not with Advisors Excel, bragged about his high service standard. He did roughly $20 million a year with an average case size of $100,000 and sold a lot of clients on his personalized service model. He claimed he was the only advisor who gave every client his cell phone number so he could personally help any client immediately—nights, weekends—whenever they needed him he would be there. Not only could clients reach him at any time, he promised to answer—or return—calls immediately.

Think about this. Based on the advisor's volume, he would accumulate 1,000 clients within five years. Imagine making and following through on that promise to 1,000 clients. Impossible. What sounded great at first, ended up being a nightmare business model. Was the personal cell phone promise necessary for the sale? Was it a crucial component of the buying decision? No. Everyone would have been better off if the advisor had set lasting expectations.

This story does not end well. Come to find out, during the first few months with a client, this advisor did what he promised to do during the sales process. However, his service took a turn for the worse a few months later. I searched this advisor on the web and discovered he had more customer complaints than any advisor I'd ever seen. Come to find out not only did he offer an unrealistic service standard, he also exaggerated product features. It's too bad. He was a gifted sales person who could have experienced real success without overpromising.

The lesson: No matter what happens, do not make promises you and your business cannot deliver.

Ditch the Headaches and Gain Loyal Clients

Expectations are the number one factor in client satisfaction and will dramatically impact your satisfaction with your own business. Set the right expectations during the sales process and instead of a long-term headache, you'll have incredible, long lasting, valuable client relationships. You will have sustainable success with clients who are not only satisfied, but who also love working with you. Make expectations work for you by always underpromising and overdelivering.

Let's look at how this worked for two advisors. Advisor One overpromised and underdelivered. Advisor Two underpromised and overdelivered. Advisor One promised clients he'd call them back within thirty minutes every time they called no matter what. The first time the client called, he was in a meeting and called her back two hours later. He overpromised and underdelivered.

Expectations are the number one
factor in client satisfaction and
will dramatically impact your
satisfaction with your own business.

Instead of promising a call back within thirty minutes, Advisor Two promised that he or a team member would call back within twenty-four hours no matter what. Not only did Advisor Two state a realistic call back time, he included his team in the promise, lessening the demands on his time. His clients accepted this timeframe and appreciated the commitment. When a client called his office and a team member returned her call in two hours, the client was thrilled. Advisor Two underpromised and overdelivered. Advisor Two exceeded client expectations because they were realistic and he could therefore go above and beyond.

When it comes to service, speed builds trust. Don't keep your clients waiting. A call back in two hours when the expectation was twenty-four hours, thrills clients and builds credibility. Always underpromise and overdeliver. Get back with the client sooner than expected.

Another key element to setting realistic expectations, is communicating how your company will service clients. If you have a team, clearly explain to clients how the team works so the client doesn't expect you to do everything. If instead, you do your own service, tell your client that immediately.

I know an advisor who will not finish a sale until he has this quick three-minute conversation with each new client. It goes like this:

"Mr. Client, I really appreciate you putting your trust and confidence in us here at XYZ Financial. We're really looking forward to working with you. If you don't mind, I'd like to share how our company is structured to give you the best experience possible. Is that fair? Okay, great.

"As you know, and have seen, we take a team approach. We've found our clients love this. It tends to lead to quicker and higher quality service. You are my priority. Whenever you need me, I'm here for you, but there will be a time when you need something and I may be in a meeting, or out of town. In that case, I can't be all things to all people. I don't want my absence to prevent you from getting what you need, so I want you to know, we have a team of professionals here to serve you. I trust them to make the same decisions I would make. You will not get inferior service when you talk with them, but if you ever need me personally, I am here for you. Does that make sense? Okay, great."

He then immediately introduces the clients to a couple of team members as well as his client service staff. This starts the relationship down the right path. Clients know they have a whole team to work with and realize they don't need to go to the advisor for everything. This approach is much more effective than if an advisor does everything themselves, or fails to tell the client about their team.

Think about it. If the advisor hadn't introduced his staff to the client, a week or two later when the client called, they'd end up in his voicemail and he would have no choice but to service their every need. And if he's unavailable? Too bad. The client is stuck waiting. Instead of everything depending on my advisor, the team is involved. This leads to a lasting client/advisor relationship.

One firm I know does a great job setting expectations. Their business model has advisors visiting clients in their homes two or three times. Once the sales process is over, clients communicate with the company's home office for all service needs. The advisor closes the business and lets clients know how service will work going forward. The client rarely talks with the advisor again. This works for one reason—the process is communicated to clients up front and they know what to expect. If the company's advisors had positioned themselves as the go-to guy or girl, this model would have been a disaster.

Assess your services by comparing them to expectations and promises you've made to clients. To meet expectations, you may need to change how quickly your team responds to emails, or phone calls. Maybe you change your system so clients always get a live person when they call instead of voicemail. Whatever the promise, match it to the expectation set. Are there any common complaints clients raise shortly after becoming a client? If so, it may mean expectations are incorrect. Make sure expectations are realistic and find ways to exceed them whenever you can.

The Hassle of Setting Unrealistic Expectations

Sometimes, advisors pay too high of a price for business, right? Often, they do this by making exceptions for clients. They deviate from business as usual to help one client.

Let's say your office is open every weekday from 8 a.m. to 5 p.m., but a top prospect wants to meet at 6:30 p.m. Do you make the exception? Many advisors will. The mature advisors won't. They refuse to mold and shape their business model to fit every client's specific needs. Clients and prospects must fit into the *advisor's* business model.

By setting the expectation that you will meet with the prospect in the evening this one time, implies that when they become a client, they can expect the same. Add a few clients with this expectation and your hours will change. A client should be willing to work with you based on your existing structure. Don't shift your business model to fit a client's needs. It's a slippery slope that most advisors end up regretting.

Setting realistic, achievable expectations from the beginning benefits the client and the practice while laying a foundation for a sustainable, enjoyable, long-term client relationship.

Chapter 21: Set Realistic Expectations

Avoid setting expectations you can't uphold by asking yourself the following:

1) What expectations do I set for clients and do they align with the service I provide?

2) Which of my expectations–for products and services—are unsustainable?

3) How can I bring the concept of underpromise and overdeliver to my practice?

22

SELL MORE WITH A TOP-NOTCH TEAM

"Talent wins games, but teamwork and
intelligence wins championships."

— *Michael Jordan*

C ount the salespeople in your office. Did you only include advisors and producers? If you did, you just undercut the actual size of your sales team.

Every person who interacts with a client on any level is a salesperson. A receptionist sells a team's friendliness, workability, and enthusiasm. A client service person sells how much your company cares for clients and how well you fulfill their needs. Every client interaction provides the entire office with a chance to help someone. Every interaction is a sales opportunity to remind the client they are in great hands. Staff, not the advisor, define a practice, its personality, and its reputation. Your staff's willingness to help clients or prospects directly impacts the perception clients have of your business.

Hire an Outstanding Gatekeeper

I've visited hundreds of advisory offices throughout the years. My first perception of an advisor's office says a lot. It speaks to how well they are staffed, how effectively they run their business, and how much attention they pay to detail. In most offices, the receptionist is the first touchpoint with the client. Consider how two different receptionists in two different offices set the tone for their clients.

First, Mary answers a call from a client named Mr. Jones. Mr. Jones has a simple request. He wants to change his appointment time. Mary is in a hurry; her voice is flat. Maybe she's having a bad day. She answers with, "Hello?"

"Hi, this is Mr. Jones. I'm wondering if I can change my appointment for tomorrow?"

"Who is your appointment with?"

"Mr. Advisor."

"I'm sorry, he's busy," Mary says. "Can he call you back?"

"Yes. Please have him call me at 555-2233."

"Okay. I'll have him call you. Bye."

Unlike Mary, the second receptionist, Megan, is calm, pleasant, professional, and helpful. When a Mr. Jones calls Megan's office, Megan says, "Thank you for calling XYZ Office, this is Megan, how may I help you?"

"Hi, this is Mr. Jones. I'm wondering if I can change my appointment for tomorrow?"

"Sure Mr. Jones," Megan says. "I'm happy to help. What day and time would work best?"

"Sometime in the afternoon on Tuesday?"

"Mr. Advisor is open at 2 p.m."

"That would be great."

"Great. Is there anything else I can assist with?"

"No."

"Well, have a great day. We look forward to seeing you soon. I'll be sure Mr. Advisor is 100 percent prepared for your visit."

Every experience a client has with your practice must be incredible.

We love receptionists and assistants. They're great firm guard dogs, but they shouldn't growl. Receptionists are the first touch-point between your firm and the client. They must be friendly, engaged, and 100 percent present. If you sell how great your team is, but your team seems careless, the client's impression is that you have a careless team. Every experience a client has with your practice must be incredible.

Client Experience		
Positive	~~Neutral~~ *Negative*	Negative

Client Perception is Everything

Perhaps your practice isn't unfriendly. Perhaps it's too casual for the image you want to project. Say a prospective client calls and gets a voicemail greeting that sounds like the advisor's home phone. "Hey, this is Joe. You know what to do."

Not only is the message cavalier, it doesn't solve the client's problem. A receptionist can answer questions and provide assistance. Helpful, polite, positive interactions are selling at its best. Unhelpful, weak or outright rude interactions are sales at its worst. I've experienced the absolute best, worst, and in-between.

In addition to projecting your image, staff is responsible for keeping clients happy no matter how crazy or unrealistic the request.

The shoe company, Zappos, excels at this. If a client heads to Las Vegas, calls Zappos, and says, "I'm not from Vegas, but am in town for fun. Can you recommend somewhere to eat?"

The Zappos representative won't say, "Sorry, we sell shoes. Good luck."

Instead, he or she will Yelp the top three Italian restaurants in Vegas, and sit on the phone until the client found a restaurant. It's a great experience.

Great advisors do this, too. Say after chatting about a beneficiary change, your client says, "We're looking to change CPAs. Can you recommend one?"

Most advisors say, "We're not in the tax business, sorry," and get the client off the phone. Like we said earlier, this business is all about helping people. Elite advisors will try to help in any way they can, regardless of the client's need. In the case of the above example, an elite advisor may recommend a trusted CPA or conference the client into an office of a CPA they know and trust. If your client needs help, find a way to help them. And by the way, we talked about listening to your clients. If this request comes in, it might tell you your clients would value a resource to help them with taxes.

I have one advisor who literally has a Rolodex of resources for clients. If a client needs a handyman for a summer project, this advisor recommends one of his clients, who is also a great handyman. Not only is this advisor great at what he does, he also connects his clients to every resource he has. He is the go-to guy for many of his clients' needs.

If your client needs help, find a way to help them.

Sometimes your reputation isn't what you think it is. Test-drive your client interactions with staff. This is a great way to get a feel for the client experience. Either pull some recorded phone calls, or have a friend call in to see if your company personality matches their interactions with staff. Note how the receptionist reacts to phone calls, how long clients sit on hold, and ask yourself if this is the reputation you hope to have with clients.

B O A R D

Chapter 22: Sell More with a Top-Notch Team

The image we think we project isn't always the same as the image we actually project. Test drive your client experience by:

1) Determining whether your staff is *really* trained to sell the experience you would like them to sell

2) Determining whether you're currently serving as a connector for your clients

3) Having a friend test drive your experience so they can report back to you

SECTION 3:
MASTER SALES
SUMMARY

S elling isn't selling. The days of hard pressure sales are gone, hopefully forever. Today, selling is all about helping people. The first step to becoming a great salesperson is learning how to be a great listener. Ask clients questions that go beyond their financial goals so you can understand where they're coming from and what solution might best work for them. Share your story with your clients in order to build a personal connection. Find ways to use dramatic demonstrations and visuals that will bring your presentation to life.

At the end of the day, we're all more or less selling similar products. A client's decision to choose you over another advisor depends entirely on your ability to sell yourself and your belief in the products, services, and support you offer. Get your team to believe in the value they provide to clients by sharing stories about how they impact clients and then encourage them to provide as much value to client as possible. Top advisors don't just offer financial advice. They connect clients to CPAs and other professionals the client needs. If there's 100 points in every sale, top advisors score 120 points because they provide so much *extra* value to clients.

During every appointment, set realistic, clear expectations with your client. Never overpromise and underdeliver; be up front about a product's benefits and terms and conditions. Fine-tune your six-step sales processes by building rapport, identifying the problem, agreeing on a problem, agreeing on a solution, validating the solution, and bulletproofing the sale. After you get a new client, start your relationship off right with lots of communication and even by sending a nice welcome package.

Look at your most common objections and figure out how to address them *during* your sales process. Assume your client wants to do business with you and offer a clear solution that's explained in terms they understand.

Understand that even though you may be the one closing the sale, every single person in your office who interacts with that client is also a salesperson. Every single one of them can make or break that client's experience. Everything you do, say, or project affects your image. Make sure that the image you project is one you're proud of. Finally, don't get better at following a sales script. Get better at helping people.

SUMMARY

Section 3: Master Sales

Top Three GO Elite Actions to Master Sales:

1) Learn to sell yourself, your team, your unique process, and your service, not just your products

2) Fine tune your six-step sales process, and get comfortable with objections

3) Add value to your clients whenever possible. This often means providing solutions that extend beyond your role as a financial advisor

MASTER OPERATIONS

"He who gains time gains everything."
— *Benjamin Disraeli*

This business is one continuous cycle. The more marketing you do, the more people you see. The more people you see, the more clients you get. The more clients you get, the more infrastructure you need to support them.

Everything you've worked so hard to grasp up this point—knowing your numbers, focusing on your mission, adding tremendous value—will fall apart if you don't master operations. This means building a great infrastructure that enables you to manage your time, trusting an outstanding staff, and providing an incredible experience for clients so you can continue growing your business.

Too many advisors learn the top strategies to succeeding in this business while sharpening the skills they need to produce well, only to hit a wall and plateau. I've worked with countless advisors who generate $300,000 or $500,000 in revenue only to sit in the office year after year with the attitude that additional growth is impossible.

Sometimes they falsely believe they've set their businesses up incorrectly and try to reinvent themselves at every turn. However, no matter what they try, they can't seem to break through to the next production level.

In almost every case, the answer to increasing production is not what these advisors should do. It lies in what they should not do.

Think about it. When you start in this business, there's nothing to do but produce. Your focus is on marketing or selling, so administrative tasks are minimal. You have more free time and little to do.

Once you add clients, demands on your time increase because you must fulfill the promises you've made. You have to take care of your new clients. Slowly but surely, clients call or email because they have questions or need help. Gradually, the time you have available for production will diminish. It makes sense that you feel you don't have any time for growth. Generally, this isn't the case. It's not that you don't have enough time to generate more business, it's that you spend too much time focused on the wrong tasks.

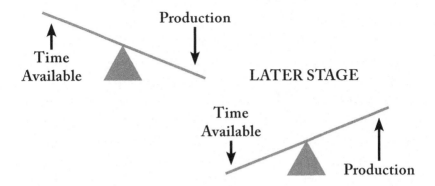

Once production increases, many advisors struggle to give up control of day-to-day activities. They have the mindset that if they want anything done correctly, they have to do it themselves. They don't have the patience to train staff to take over, or they feel they owe it to their clients to do everything themselves. Pretty soon, a day on the calendar devoted to marketing and selling is spent servicing clients and dealing with administrative issues. Instead of focusing on skilled tasks, these advisors start doing low-value tasks. Their schedule revolves around meeting the needs of others, rather than on enjoying the high value activities they should be doing.

A critical way to examine the relationship between time and money is to consider how much an hour of your time is worth to your business. If your annual revenue is $300,000 and you work forty hours a week fifty weeks a year, what's an hour of your time worth to your business?

40 hours/week x 50 weeks/year = 2,000 hours

$300,000/2000 hours = $150/hour

The skillset you've developed to get your company where it is today is worth $150 per hour worked. Here's a question. Would you pay someone $150 an hour to do the little tasks that take you away from your core activities? Tasks like answering phones or making coffee? Most advisors would say no, that's *way* too expensive.

What would it cost to have someone else handle administrative needs while also offering great service to your clients? Depending on the responsibilities, you're looking at $15 to $30 an hour. This is much less costly than paying you $150 an hour to do the same. If you have twenty hours a week of low-value tasks that can be handed to someone else for $15 to $30 an hour, you have more free time to do what you do best at $150 an hour. Not only will this impact your bottom line, it will keep you fresh for those valuable clients.

I ran through this idea of personal worth with one of my advisors. We found that when he was in the office, his time was worth $250 an hour. We found that on average, he spent nine hours per week prospecting, which included any activity that put him in front of prospects—speaking at an event, meeting with people for the first time, or talking to someone who was coming in for another sales appointment. During these nine hours of prospecting, he generated $27,000 in revenue. For this advisor, prospecting activities were worth $3,000 per hour. His highest-value activity was worth more than $3,000 an hour. Every one of us has has $1,000-, $2,000-, or $3,000-an-hour activities. We just don't spend enough time doing them.

Think about it. If a professional basketball player says he works fifty hours a week, but only two of those hours are spent on the court, his overall performance and value will decrease. The same goes for financial advisors. A financial advisor who works eighty hours a week but only spends five hours with clients will struggle to reach his goals because he's working hard, not smart.

When it comes to appointments, for the majority of advisors, working smart directly correlates to hours of weekly face time with new clients. In fact, for 99 percent of advisors, seeing more people is the single answer to increasing business. Seeing more people is the bottom line.

Value vs. Task

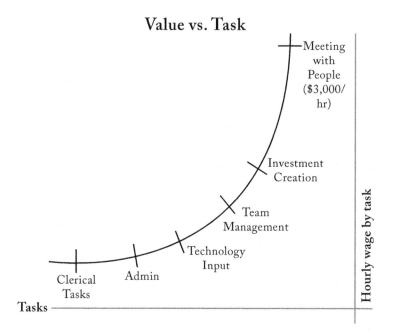

Many financial advisors work fifty hours a week, but if they have five one-hour appointments, only five hours of that fifty hours is spent with clients. Seeing more people is the goal for most advisors, so this work model isn't the path to achievement. You can feel like a hard worker and have pride in how many hours you work each week, but if it's spent on the wrong activities, it's not productive work that will grow your business and increase production.

There's nothing sadder than watching somebody work as hard as they can on tasks that don't lead to the outcome they desire. They are so busy doing things in the here and now that they don't need to do, that they fail to do the things that will impact their future goals. This is a choice. Don't choose to focus on low-value activities. Instead, focus on what will give you a better tomorrow. Too often today's needs win that battle, and advisors walk into a hamster wheel of day-to-day survival. They never give themselves the chance to focus on what matters most.

I know a few advisors who have outgrown their need to see people. They do so well marketing and bringing in clients that their time is better spent focusing on marketing. They actually have other qualified advisors meet with people for them, a topic we'll talk about in greater detail in chapter twenty-four.

Say one of these advisors is able to generate forty appointments a week. Even if they're the best salesperson in the office and have a 40 percent closing ratio, they can't meet with all forty people. They don't have enough time in the week so they settle on just meeting with twenty people per week. At a 40 percent closing ratio, they are able to bring in eight new clients per week.

Say this advisor creates a team of four advisors and starts creating forty appointments per week for them, ten per advisor. If those advisors aren't as good at sales as he is, and only have a 30 percent closing ratio, they still, as a group, bring on twelve new clients per week versus the eight he could bring on himself. In this case, if our advisor focuses on building out advisors and marketing, his business is more scalable than if he spends all his time meeting clients on his own. He actually grows so much he outgrows his role.

However wonderful this scenario sounds, it is rare that an advisor reaches this stage. Of the thousands of advisors I've met with, this scenario applies to fewer than twenty.

Most advisors need to focus on seeing more people themselves, but there is a chance your priority activities will change as your business grows and evolves. The busier you get, the better you have to prioritize your schedule so you can focus on the right things. The better you prioritize your time, the better your productivity. Productivity without priority is not productive.

Often times, one of the first questions I ask a new advisor is, "What's the one thing that can substantially increase your business over the next twelve months?"

This question forces advisors to think about the most important factors of their business. It helps specify which tasks will immediately make the biggest difference in their business. Often times, by accomplishing that one thing, advisors find that the little things matter less.

After new advisors share their one thing, I ask, "Since that one thing is so important to your business's success, how much time do you spend doing that one thing each day? How about each week?"

Productivity without priority
is not productive.

The answers are incredible. Most advisors spend 90 percent of their time doing anything but that one thing. They get side tracked by client service, paperwork, calling insurance companies, and checking emails. Before long, the definition of what they spend their time doing has completely changed. Had they freed up more of their time, they would have been able to keep doing what made them successful in the first place. Your key to doubling your business is doubling the time you have available on your calendar to do what you do best.

Learn to delegate, hire outstanding people, project an image to clients that supports your service, and watch how much more productive you will be.

OBJECTIVES

Section 4: Master Operations

In this section, you will learn how to:

- Focus on your strengths and delegate all other tasks
- Live by your calendar
- Hire and support awesome staff
- Protect your business
- Provide outstanding proactive and reactive services
- Get clients excited about working with your entire team
- Create a personalized, positive, impact culture
- Develop an image that supports the one you want to project
- Support charities to support your business
- Develop a referral-based business
- Increase production by hiring an associate advisor

23

ESTABLISH A TEAM THAT HELPS YOU WIN BIG

"Deciding what not to do is as important
as finding out what to do."

— *Steve Jobs*

The single most important factor for building a great business is building a great team. People spend far too much time working on tasks that do not fall within their core skill set. In this business, the breadth of your accomplishments is heavily dependent on how well you develop a great team so that you can focus on what you do best. No one person can accomplish as much as a great team. This business is not a solo mission. Nobody wins big alone.

Play to Your Strengths

I work with an advisor named Kyle. He is the most likeable guy you'll ever meet. He's that guy in the room whom everyone's drawn to. He's a great guy, a people person, and everyone loves him. While

Kyle is top-notch with people—he's funny and incredibly fun to hang out with—unfortunately, he's really unorganized and so much of a people pleaser that it actually hurts his business.

Kyle knows his stuff. He brings in clients and does a great job taking care of them. However, a few years ago, he said his office was a complete mess. A close review showed 99 percent of Kyle's paperwork was incorrect. Kyle would fill out the paperwork, send it in, get it back for corrections, and send it in again. He thought that was a normal part of business. It turns out that he never asked his qualified employees to complete the paperwork for him. In fact, he never asked much of his employees at all. They were his friends. He asked them for favors from time to time, but was too focused on keeping staff happy to actually ask them to do things they didn't want to do. He dreaded confrontation and was a people pleaser, so he never really got onto his staff for what they did wrong either.

Kyle recognized that his current business model wasn't working so he developed a business to support both his strengths and weaknesses. Because Kyle is great with people, he developed a practice that allowed him to spend the majority of his time in front of people. Instead of trying to improve on weaknesses such as paperwork, Kyle hired people whose strengths compensated for his weakness. He hired a key office manager who took 90 percent of the administrative tasks off his plate, including staff management. Kyle stopped setting up his own events, which gave him time and energy to charm the crowd. Kyle had employees do all the activities that had been holding him back.

As a result, business grew off the charts and was a lot more fun for Kyle because he was able to do the things he enjoyed. Successful advisors like Kyle build businesses that allow them to spend the majority of their time focusing on their strengths and delegate the rest.

Escape Productivity-Killing Distractions

Many advisors feel they owe it to clients to personally react to their every need. This creates a business of constant disruption where it's impossible to focus on anything. As soon as these advisors start a project, a client calls with a question or an account update. No business professional can work productively when they react to the needs of others and let others control their time. You've got to have a structure in place to support your schedule and protect your valuable time so you can focus on what's most important. The cost of a great service person is much less than the cost of you *not* focusing on the elements most important to your business. Having a supportive team makes for a better, more efficient business.

This idea applies to every industry. Let's look at doctors. If a family practitioner had to answer the phone, deal with the files, and schedule appointments, when would he have time to see you?

Doctors never spend the whole visit with a patient. The receptionist checks the patient in and manages the paperwork. The nurse takes the patient's blood pressure and other vitals so that by the time the doctor sees the patient, the groundwork for the visit has been laid. At that point, the patient has interacted with at least two other team members. During the visit, the doctor will likely ask the nurse, receptionist, or medical student about a certain condition, or about the patient's history. It's not that the doctor couldn't do those things himself, it's that he understands the greatest impact he has is spending time with the patient face-to-face in order to diagnose the problem. This is beneficial to the patient, who not only receives the doctor's full attention, but who also receives attention from staff members who are also focused on their high-value activities as well. Imagine if the doctor took the vitals, answered the phones, and looked up prescriptions. Nothing would get done.

Patients get the most value from their doctor when the doctor doesn't work as an individual, but as a team. If the team works together and each member plays to his or her strengths, the patient receives the best care. The same goes for financial services.

Make Your Business Extraordinary

Let's say a patient works 9 a.m. to 5:30 p.m. and cannot get to the doctor's office before it closes at five. If that patient were adamant and said, "Listen doc, I have to see you today even if it's not until 6:30 p.m." Would that patient get good service if the doctor stayed knowing his full team had already left for the day? Probably not. No matter how smart or capable the doctor is, his productivity is reliant on his team.

Success is as much about what you don't do as it is about what you do. If you want to be extraordinary, you have to say no to average things. You've got to learn to prioritize your schedule, focus on what you should be doing, and build a great team that's capable of doing everything else. This will increase production, make for a more fulfilling workday, and lead to happier clients.

> Success is as much about what you don't do as it is about what you do. If you want to be extraordinary, you have to say no to average things.

B   O   A   R   D

Chapter 23: Establish a Team That Helps You Win Big

You need an incredible team to help you reach your goals. Be sure to:

1) Build a great team around you

2) Hire people that can overcompensate for your weaknesses

3) Create a culture where your employees work to protect your time so you can focus on what's most important

24

AVOID THE ADVISOR CURSE

"Where focus goes, energy flows. And
if you don't take the time to focus
on what matters, then you're living
a life of someone else's design."

— *Tony Robbins*

Remember the advisor who hated marketing because he refused to let staff help set up his seminars? He suffered from what I call The Advisor Curse—a perfectionist's need to control—that great advisors should resist at all costs. The problem with the curse is that it's the source of most time management issues. Advisors who can't let go and delegate can't focus on their highest-value activities. To avoid The Advisor Curse, you've got to hire, train, and trust your team. You've got to put low-value activities aside and focus on what you do best.

Imagine if Richard Branson, who owns 400 companies, had to manage every aspect of every company. He has so many companies, that there are not enough days in the year for him devote even one day to each company. So how does he do it? He hires great people to run his businesses for him. If he can do that, there is nothing you can't delegate within your business. You really shouldn't do yourself what others can do for you at a cheaper cost. Examples like this are prevalent among successful people in all industries.

Let's take a lesson from the sports world. Ted Williams was the last baseball player to bat over 400, making him one of the greatest hitters of all time. His secret? He only swung at the right pitches, and he knew exactly which pitches were the right ones. Williams calculated his own strike zone into seventy-seven cells, each the size of a baseball. His sweet spot included nine of those cells. Pitches that hit any of the remaining sixty-eight cells drastically lowered his probability of success.

Imagine how many balls passed through those sixty-eight cells. Instead of swinging away, Williams patiently waited for the balls to land in his nine sweet spot zones. True, Williams could have spent less time working on the miracle nine and more time practicing hitting pitches outside his optimal zone, but he chose to focus on his sweet spot. The results speak for themselves.

Strike Zone

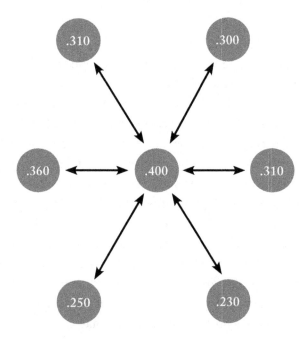

Top advisors do with their businesses what Williams did in baseball. They know a lot about everything, but they never try to do it all. They focus the majority of their time on their sweet spot.

Clients' needs are endless, so advisors find themselves wearing too many hats. One minute the advisor is an income planner, the next minute he's a life insurance salesman. Top advisors don't do this. They find their personal sweet spots and delegate the remaining sixty-eight tasks to other people in their office.

A Quick Way to Immediately Boost Your Bottom Line

Just like Williams, you only have so many cells of time in your calendar. Your job is to fill those cells with your highest-value activities. You can only grow as big as your calendar can stretch. Your calendar can only stretch if you prioritize what activities fill it.

You can only grow as big as
your calendar can stretch. Your
calendar can only stretch if you
prioritize what activities fill it.

Here's how to do it. Let's say income planning averages $1,000 an hour, term life insurance $250 an hour, long term care $200 an hour, and Med Supps $50 an hour. Oftentimes, advisors say they're too busy to see income planning prospects because of something like a long term care case. So they have a long term care case that's valued at $200 an hour, take the spot of an income planning appointment which is worth $1,000 an hour. The advisor is essentially stepping over dollars to pick up pennies. The advisor swings at a pitch outside of their optimal zone.

What pitches are in your optimal zone?

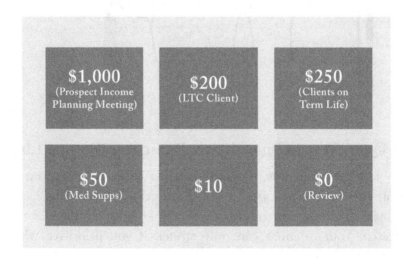

This doesn't mean you shouldn't help clients with long-term care or other lower value services, you just shouldn't personally switch gears to be a long-term care salesperson when you could be focused on higher-value activities. Help clients with added value services by having a qualified team member handle it or by referring them to someone who specializes in that area. After all, if that type of work isn't in your optimal zone, who's to say it isn't in theirs?

During the marketing and sales sections, we talked about increasing your income by creating more individual sales and writing larger case sizes. Chasing more sales can lead to burnout. Getting bigger sales is a great goal, but it takes time. Guess what? There's a third, more immediate way to increase your income and we've got Williams to thank for it. Make more revenue per sale. Instead of writing long term care for $200 an hour, narrow your focus and fill your calendar exclusively with $1,000 per hour work. Quit doing everything, focus on excelling at your highest-priority tasks, and build a great team to handle everything else.

Let's look at another great example in a totally different industry—the late Steve Jobs, genius and co-founder of Apple, one of the most innovative companies in the world. Jobs was the face of Apple; however, I never called Jobs when I had trouble with my iPhone. We knew better than to expect Jobs to answer all of the little service requests customers had, right? Had he tried to do everything himself, had he had this curse, how big would Apple have gotten?

If Jobs focused on low-value activities such as customer service, instead of high-value activities such as innovation, he wouldn't have been the head of Apple. He would have been a small computer manufacturer.

Like Jobs, you are the head of your organization. You've got to be picky about how you spend your time. Narrow your focus, swing at the right pitch, and crush it.

The Difference Between 6-Figure and 7-Figure Earners

Narrowing your focus is the biggest difference between advisors who bring in millions of dollars in revenue a year and those who bring in hundreds of thousands of dollars a year.

> Narrowing your focus is the
> biggest difference between
> advisors who bring in millions
> of dollars in revenue a year and
> those who bring in hundreds of
> thousands of dollars a year.

Think about it. Both advisors have the same amount of available time. In my experience, often times both have very similar skillsets, so their level of success comes down to how well they use their time. Time is money. I've seen advisors triple their income within a year. Did their skillset change? Maybe a little, but enough to make that significant of a change? I don't think so. These advisors changed how they spent their time and their businesses flourished as a result.

Too many advisors think if they want to do something right, they have to do it themselves so they end up caught up in minutia that doesn't produce anything. The reason this happens—and I hate to say it—is that too many advisors are control freaks. Top advisors are fine with someone else doing something 90 percent as well as they would have done it. I'm not saying you can't train people to do things your way—you can—but I'd challenge you to let the staff do things their way. Chances are, the person you're delegating to will do that task better than you because it's one of the things they do best.

Think of it this way. One of my advisor friends creates $30 to $40 million a year in new assets. Now, if he answered the phone, managed accounts, provided annual reviews, set up seminars, took out the trash, developed new marketing materials, and scheduled appointments, how would he see clients? He wouldn't.

This advisor delegates so well, he answered one of my midmorning calls about a business opportunity from the tennis court. He said, "Shawn, you know I don't get into the office until ten."

The same thing happens in the afternoon—he's out by three. How does he produce so much more than most advisors while working from 10 a.m. to 3 p.m.? He's a master delegator. When he arrives at the office, he gets a clipboard of notes and literally walks into a meeting with a client who has already talked to one of his team members. He walks in to do what he does best, meets back-to-back with five clients, goes home, and has fun. He produces more than most advisors in less time, and his business gives him phenomenal amounts of freedom. Learn to delegate and you can have this, too.

Don't Know What to Delegate? Try This Exercise

Write down everything you do in a week. If you get in at 8 a.m. and brew coffee, write it down. If at 9:30 a.m., you schedule your clients, write it down. This may sound crazy, but record every single activity you do in a week. Now, look at that list. How many of those activities are worth your hourly wage? If making coffee is on that list, come down and make me a cup because at $250 an hour, it must be the best cup ever made. Now for the real test. How many of those hours were spent with marketing or prospective clients? Five? Ten?

If you worked fifty hours that week and only five were spent with clients, you're not focusing on the right activities. Ninety percent of everything else on your to-do list can be done by someone else. Identify each item on the list. How many hours could you save on your calendar by eliminating those low-value tasks? Note who in the office could take that task off of your plate and which items could you delegate but are not currently delegating. If there are a lot of these tasks, you've just created a job description for a new employee.

I had an advisor who was working fifty hours a week. He was frustrated with his growth because it had plateaued. We went through this exercise and he agreed to hire an assistant full time at $15 an hour so he could see the ten clients he needed to see a week to meet his production goals. Before the hire, he only saw five clients a week because he "didn't have time" to see more. The new hire gave him twenty-five extra hours a week to market and see clients. Guess what? His production increased dramatically.

When you delegate, do what this advisor did and do it permanently. Train existing or new staff well so they can take the task, run with it, and even train someone else to do it in their absence.

Train existing or new staff well
so they can take the task, run
with it, and train someone else
to do it in their absence.

Take a look at this chart of seventy things to delegate. What do you delegate? What can you delegate?

Place an "X" in the box that represents who in your office performs each of these tasks.
(**P** - Producer   **S** - Staff/team member   **N/A** - Non-applicable)

Clerical	P	S	N/A	Administrative	P	S	N/A
Answering phone calls	☐	☐	☐	Tracking licensing requirements	☐	☐	☐
Scheduling appointments	☐	☐	☐	Tracking transfer process	☐	☐	☐
Composing letters	☐	☐	☐	Processing trades*	☐	☐	☐
Requesting paperwork	☐	☐	☐	Researching securities*	☐	☐	☐
Opening mail	☐	☐	☐	Rebalancing portfolios*	☐	☐	☐
Completing new client account paperwork	☐	☐	☐	Resolving client concerns	☐	☐	☐
Following up on paperwork	☐	☐	☐	Composing/mailing follow-up letters to clients	☐	☐	☐
Obtaining compliance approval for letters	☐	☐	☐				
Resolving compliance issues	☐	☐	☐	Updating outside vendor contact list	☐	☐	☐
Managing client files	☐	☐	☐	Tracking commissions	☐	☐	☐
Updating office contact list	☐	☐	☐	Contacting clients about Required Minimum Distributions (RMDs), account debits, etc.	☐	☐	☐
Making coffee	☐	☐	☐				
Preparing snacks	☐	☐	☐				
Taking out trash	☐	☐	☐	Handling clients' check requests	☐	☐	☐
Typing agenda for staff meetings	☐	☐	☐	Making bank deposits	☐	☐	☐
				Sending packages	☐	☐	☐
Taking notes during staff meetings	☐	☐	☐	Creating newsletter/ e-newsletter for clients	☐	☐	☐

*Not applicable to insurance-only producers

I did this weekly activities test with another advisor who said she didn't have enough time to see clients. We realized she spent more than two hours on each appointment she had. She spent twenty minutes preparing for each one and then a half hour typing notes after the client left. For this advisor, time spent on appointments was close to twice what it should have been. She ended up hiring an assistant to take notes for her at $15 an hour, cutting her appointment time down. As an added bonus, that near hour of work my advisor did preparing and cleaning up cost $15 instead of $250. Incredible. The harsh reality is, too many advisors fall victim to doing the wrong tasks, and their businesses suffer as a result. In order to build the business you want, you've got to learn to be a master delegator.

While it's best to delegate within your office, some things can be outsourced. For example, I use a dictation service—Mobile Assistant—to take notes. I talk, the notes are recorded, transcribed, and sent to me electronically. Hiring an accountant to do accounting stuff, or an editor to help write a book, lets someone else focus on their right activity so you can focus on yours.

Hire an Associate Advisor

As I mentioned before, you may grow your business and become more and more successful, which will increase your hourly wage. As this happens, there may be a point where some of the things you do today will no longer be high-value tasks for you. Again, you may outgrow some of your responsibilities. I shared an example where one advisor got so good at marketing that he had too many people to see and couldn't handle all of the appointments himself. In that case, meeting with prospective clients was actually something he needed to delegate so he could focus his time on marketing. This was a perfect example of a time when it made sense to bring on a high quality associate advisor to increase his bandwidth.

Think about it this way. If you personally reach capacity by seeing twenty people a week, an associate advisor who can *also* see twenty clients that week *doubles* your practice's capacity. Ten associate advisors mean 200 appointments a week and an increase of hundreds of millions in production.

When you do this, the associate advisor should function like a clone. They should shadow your appointments for three to six months while you groom them on your sales processes, your value to clients and—most importantly—your mission.

Once the associate is fully trained, and you are confident they get it, get out of the way. They may not be on your level yet, but they'll get there with experience.

As one advisor I know says: "You've gotta let 'em get their nose bloody."

Start the new associate off with lower-value meetings such as client reviews. Have them service C clients or hand over prospects with less than your average client in terms of investible assets. Create a plan for the associate and communicate it so everyone is on the same page. Give the associate a chance to succeed. Do not set your business up for failure by having them learn the ropes with your most high-value prospects or the most complex cases.

You are successful because of what you've done already. Don't expect the associate to contribute the same. In the beginning, their closing ratio will likely be lower than yours. Expect that, and keep working with top prospects yourself. Even if an associate advisor doesn't add as much value initially, they still add value. Even if you have a 50 percent closing ratio, if you have two advisors with closing ratios of 30 percent each, total production is greater than production achieved on your own.

Train your associate advisors well and eventually you may have a business that will grow on its own, without you having to be there.

Take Control of Your Time

Time is money. You can get more money, but you can't really get more time, right? It's diminishing every single second that goes by, something we really can't control. However, you can control how much you get done in the time you have. And you can control how much free time you have available to you.

Think about it this way, let's say you have to make ten contacts with clients this afternoon, and to get those ten contacts done, it takes you about an hour. What if another person in your office can do that for you? Then you've just purchased, or paid for, an hour of free time because you gave the task to someone else to do. This is a simple concept, but it's the way people increase their productivity and accomplish things that most people don't think are possible.

Delegating puts you in control of your own time; however, when you schedule high-priority activities, you need to time-block. Whatever time you block must be protected at all costs. Disruptions will happen. Fires will start. Protect your time. Every time you're interrupted, it costs you a minimum of fifteen minutes in productivity. That means four interruptions knock an hour off your day. An hour. What did we determine an hour of your time is worth?

> Every time you're interrupted, it costs you a minimum of fifteen minutes in productivity. That means four interruptions knock an hour off your day.

Getting interrupted while focusing on a task, then having to switch gears and focus on the new task, then going back to the original task again is like texting and driving. When you text and drive, you're not good at driving and you're not good at texting. The same goes for multitasking in the office. If you're sort of doing one thing while sort of doing another, you're doing neither well. This kills productivity. You've got to maintain focus.

Top advisors refuse to get tugged in different directions because they're too focused on giving their full attention to core tasks. They block off time on the calendar for every single thing they must do in a day, and when it's time to do that task, they focus on it 100 percent. No interruptions. No distractions. These advisors live by the calendar.

Now, regardless of how well you've delegated, delegation isn't perfect. Staff and office issues will arise and you will have to deal with them. Your team will need guidance from time to time. To keep them from disrupting productivity, work time for them into your calendar.

Start by working two, fifteen-minute periods of time into your calendar daily—one in the morning, one in the afternoon. Let staff know they should come to you with any issues during one of those fifteen-minute periods. If no one bothers you during those time slots, knock off catch up items.

Next, during the last ten minutes of every day, meet with your team and discuss, help with, and wrap up any outstanding issues. Every Monday, schedule a sixty-minute team meeting—no cell phones allowed—and discuss items that may become interruptions. Keep the tone positive, and track and discuss items such as year-to-date production, opportunities, marketing, client calls and contacts, calendar review, pending business review, and imperative accomplishment. Those sixty minutes will set the tone for the week, put a stop to certain issues before they start, and ensure that you're not interrupted while working on the right activities.

B   O   A   R   D

Chapter 24: Avoid the Advisor Curse

When it comes to filling your calendar, don't stumble over dollars to pick up pennies.

1) Make more revenue per sale by focusing on filling your calendar exclusively with your highest-value work

2) Hire an assistant to do low-value activities so you can focus on doing what you do best

3) Let staff do the things they're good at their way— don't micromanage

4) Consider hiring an associate advisor to increase the sales capacity of your business

25

EMPOWER
YOUR TEAM

"Always treat your employees exactly as you
want them to treat your best customers."
— *Stephen R. Covey*

How much you accomplish in this business is highly dependent on how well you create a great team. It doesn't matter how focused you are or how well you delegate if you don't have a great team to delegate to. Your employees are not liabilities. They aren't expenses. They are investments. A good teammate is worth more than any other asset. Your success is determined by how well you manage and improve that asset.

Every Employee is Critical to Success

A top business coach, Darren Hardy, once asked several advisors and me, "Who are the most crucial people in your business? The people who, if not taken care of, will lead to the collapse of your business?"

Every advisor said, "My clients."

The coach said, "No, it's your staff. If your staff left you, your business would be nothing, regardless of how well you treat clients."

Treat your team like you do your best customers. When every staff member is not only on their game, but also surrounded by other high-quality team members, you'll run a better business and wow clients. A superstar advisor with a terrible staff will struggle to attract and retain clients.

Top advisors create stable organizations where employees feel respected and valued. They understand each employee has hitched a wagon to their vision and the advisor has communicated that vision to them clearly and articulately. Your vision should not be complicated. In fact, it should fit on a cocktail napkin.

Your team has to buy into your vision. If they don't, no one will achieve the outcomes you've set. One of my favorite Bible verses—Proverbs 29:18—captures this point perfectly. It says, "Where there is no vision, the people will perish." This is true, but so is the converse scenario. Where there are no people, the vision will perish.

Build a great team that buys into your vision, and your success will be endless. People want to be a part of something bigger than themselves. Your company—your vision—can be that for your employees.

Providing a strong vision, understanding employees have their own obligations and desires to fulfill, and providing a respectful environment for employees to succeed in is key to becoming a top advisor.

The First Step in Designing a Winning Team

First and foremost, you've got to hire the right people. Always hire before you need to and have a bigger team than you think you need so you can grow into them. So many people hire from behind. By the time new staff are hired and trained, it's too late, and the rest of the team is overworked. Instead, hire ahead, and hire quality people. Even though high-quality hires cost more than low-quality hires, they will provide more value. Pay employees above the going rate for their position, and give them more benefits so they have an incentive to stay. Don't try to fill a full-time void by bringing in a cheap, part-time worker such as an intern. You need A+ people. Carefully choose the people you bring into your practice. If there comes a point where you realize they're not a good fit, let them go.

As one of Advisors Excel's top advisors always says, "Be slow to hire and quick to fire."

It's much more costly to hire, then fire, then hire again. Take your time, and find the right person up front, and you'll be much better off. At the same time, as soon as you realize someone isn't doing a good job or they just aren't cut out for their position, it's probably best to find someone who is. A key question to ask yourself in this situation is: If I knew what I know now when I hired them, would I hire them again? If the answer is no, that's probably all you need to know. Having the right people is critical to your success.

> It's much more costly to hire, then
> fire, then hire again. Take your time
> and, find the right person up front
> and you'll be much better off.

As Jim Collins, author of *Good to Great* says, getting the right people on the bus and the wrong people off the bus is harder than it looks. However, this is critical to developing a strong team. Employees who are not a good fit can negatively impact morale, decrease productivity, and generally upend a team.

Don't Let One Bad Apple Ruin the Bunch

I heard this story about an advisor who hired an employee, moved her and her family across the country, and then, after a couple of months, asked the woman to leave. The relationship just didn't work. It was difficult, but it was the best decision for the employee, the advisor, and the rest of the team.

An employee who doesn't fit your team can be like a cancer. Their attitude can impact everyone and can turn a highly motivated, impactful team, into an unmotivated group of people who come to the office every day and just go through the motions.

The moment you feel an employee isn't the right fit, address it. There's a reason you have that feeling, and if you don't address it quickly, you'll kick yourself nine months down the road.

I had an advisor who waited six months after he knew his associate, Mike, was the wrong fit to broach the subject with him. When my advisor finally approached Mike to let him know it wasn't working, Mike said, "Why did it take you so long?

Mike had been struggling for months. He knew he wasn't doing what needed doing. This made him feel terrible, so he dreaded going to work each day. Mike kept the job because it was stable, but spent that entire six months feeling like he was a burden to my advisor. Every day he sat around waiting for my advisor to fire him. Every day Mike went to work feeling like a square peg in a round hole. My advisor felt terrible. He and Mike parted on good terms, and my advisor became a mentor to Mike. Remember, just because someone isn't a good fit for your office doesn't mean you can't end on good terms.

Carefully consider every hire. Be meticulous and slow in your hiring process. Be clear on what's expected, and provide all the resources the new hire needs to be successful. As soon as you know someone isn't cut out for the job, let them go. Don't drag it out. This is one of the most important things you can do for A+ employees. A+ employees want to work with other A+ employees. They don't want to make up for a C employee's lack of effort, abilities, or inattention to detail. Carefully considering every hire tells A+ employees you respect their time and will not compromise or dilute their efforts.

Get the Most Out of Your Staff

When you build your great team, accept that you will have to work with different personality and communication styles. One of my top advisors is really good at this. Not only does she realize each team member is vastly different in how they think, problem solve, and contribute to the office, she understands they all communicate differently. Some respond well to criticism; others are hyper sensitive to it. Some employees want face-to-face conversations; others prefer a one-line email. If you understand how your employees work, you'll get more out of them.

If you understand how your employees work, you'll get more out of them.

So how do you do this? Before you hire someone, have the candidate take a personality or aptitude test such as the DISC Test, Kolbe A Index/Instinct Test, or the Prevue Assessment. These can be given to existing team members as well.

HOW DO YOU DO THIS?

1) DISC Test

2) Kolbe A Index

3) Prevue Assessment

The DISC Test is a quick, five-to-ten minute test that provides insights into how you can communicate with different personality types more effectively. With your results, you can immediately improve interpersonal communications, connect with co-workers, and understand how to have more successful employee interactions.

The Kolbe A Index assesses natural instincts to measure what employees will or won't do. This thirty-six-question test is a brilliant way to get a better understanding of how you can maximize the potential output of each team member.

The Prevue Assessment measures twenty different aptitudes that give insights into personality types, general abilities, and interests. The test delves deeply into each area to provide a comprehensive look at how well the candidate fits the job and company culture.

These tests take the guesswork out of understanding your employees' communication styles, strengths, and weaknesses and outline how to improve productivity by speaking their language.

Understanding your team members' most effective modes of communication can pay tremendous dividends for the overall efficiency and effectiveness of your business. More importantly, it can play a huge role in office morale, overall buy-in, and the development of a sense of team in which staff feel they are working together toward a common goal.

Really Care for Employees, and Show You Care

Now that you know how each team member communicates, get to know them outside of work, and develop a personal relationship with them. What are they struggling with? What motivates them? What are the names of their kids? You don't need to know everything, but the more you know, the more they see you care and the more they buy into your vision.

I learned this firsthand a few years ago. I got a call from one of my advisor's staff members. She said, "Shawn, the advisor doesn't care about me. He doesn't even know my kids' names. I don't think he knows anything about my husband. He doesn't care about me as a person. I'm just there to work for him and he only cares about his business."

She ranted and raved about the experience. I was totally shocked. I couldn't believe that of all the things related to business that she could have complained about, she was most bothered that her boss didn't know her personally. Unfortunately, she ended the conversation by telling me she'd just resigned. She was a critical component of that team, yet she left over something that had nothing to do with the business. That asset found another home.

It's critical to remember that, as an employer, you are the one person outside your employees' families and friends who will have the biggest impact on their life. How you treat your employees and the culture you provide for them will dramatically impact their well-being as well as their personal and professional fulfillment.

Think about it. What happens when your employees have a great day? How do they react at home? What if they have a terrible day? How does that affect their home life? How you treat your employees and whether they dread coming into work or wake up excited to go in every day affects every facet of their life.

Whether you believe it or not, you have the power to influence your employees' marriages, their relationship with their kids, and their psychological well-being. This is a *huge* responsibly, but if you use it in a positive way, you can be an incredible asset to your employees.

Keep Your Staff Motivated

Everyone needs a vision for the future—something to move toward—so get to know your employees and share your hopes and dreams for your business with them. We spend so much time showing clients love, but employees need love, too.

> We spend so much time showing clients love, but employees need love, too.

One of our advisors starts his week with an all-staff meeting. He literally goes around the table and has everyone share something positive that's happening in their lives. They also share something positive that's happening in the business world. Maybe they talk about a goal the company just achieved, or an uptick in the economy. It's a great way to get to know employees, let employees know him, and start the week on a positive note. It also opens employees up to sharing more feedback and gives them a glimpse into the why behind your mission.

Discuss where your company is headed and why it's headed there. This gives meaning to the expectations set for each employee. Take twenty to thirty minutes in your next meeting and cover your vision and present direction with your team. While both may be clear in *your* head, they may be muddy in the minds of your staff.

If possible, hone in on a recent business decision where results are to be determined. Share the decision with your team, explain the rationale behind it, and confess that you don't know exactly how it's going to turn out. This willingness to share a potentially vulnerable aspect of your business will help staff buy into results and give them greater ownership in strategy and execution of goals.

As Vince Lombardi said, "It's hard to be aggressive when you are confused."

Be clear about everything. Make sure everyone is on the same page so you all know what you're fighting for.

Introduce Your Team to Your Clients

As we discussed earlier, never start a relationship with a client by saying, "I'm your man" or "I'm your woman." This tells the client they can expect to work with you and only you. Start by introducing them to your incredible team.

When you talk about your business, say we instead of I. Not only will clients embrace the team spirit, they'll love it. They'll love the personal attention they get from not only you, but from everyone in your office. It leaves the impression that whatever they need, it's all hands on deck.

If you have a few clients who will only work with you, wean them from this dependency by gradually introducing them to your team. Before your next meeting, ask the client if they mind if you have a team member join you for the meeting. Train your team to offer help on the phone. If you're not available, have them say, "I'm sorry, but Mr. Advisor is currently away from his desk. We'd like to help you as soon as possible. Is there anything I can do for you?"

This weaning process must be done carefully. Over time, difficult clients will open up to, and even appreciate, your team approach.

When advisors start this process, I often suggest that they send clients a team welcome letter letting the client know they'll be managed not by one person, but by a whole group. This enhances the client relationship, gives clients access to more resources, and prevents overwhelming any single staff member. No matter how you introduce clients to the team, the idea is that the team adds value. Your clients will trust you no matter what. The real prize is in handing that trust to your team, which leads to a sustainable, thriving business.

One of our advisors actually requires that every new employee sit in and experience client meetings. This advisor wants their employees to see and feel what it's like when a client is in tears because they just found out they will be able to retire, or is desperate for financial help because their spouse just passed and they don't know what to do. These experiences ensure that employees completely understand the importance of their job and how big of a role they play in their clients' lives. This makes them fall in love with the business just like the advisors have themselves.

B   O   A   R   D

Chapter 25: Empower Your Team

Great teams build great businesses. Build your team by:

1) Using personality tests to decipher their preferred communication styles

2) Ensuring your hiring process is designed to bring A+ people into your office

3) Developing a meeting structure that creates a more open, positive workplace

4) Always using we instead of I when talking to clients about your business

26

DEVELOP
A WINNING
CULTURE

"Clients do not come first. Employees come
first. If you take care of your employees,
they will take care of the clients."

— *Richard Branson*

Now that we've discussed sharing your vision and empowering your employees, it's time to discuss proper incentives that will get them going to the next level.

Want to make an investment that will yield a 10:1 return? Invest in your team. First and foremost, this means providing basic benefits such as a 401(k), paid time off, and health insurance. You may take these perks for granted, but they're a huge deal to employees and are critical to keep good staff. Next, think about providing unexpected incentives.

In 2014, seven of Advisor Excel's producers promised employees a company trip for hitting stretch goals. Coincidence or not, every single office hit that goal for a success rate of 100 percent. How's that for a probability of success?

While planning a company trip may sound daunting—and expensive—it doesn't have to be. All-inclusive trips to a place like

Cancun costs about $3,000 to $4,000 a couple, so if you have five staff, that's 15,000 to $20,000. To pay for that, answer this question. How much more production would your team need to hit to pay for a $15,000 or $20,000 trip?

If your goal is $15 million, post flyers around the office and put up a goal meter so staff is constantly reminded what they're working toward. Staff will start coming in earlier, working harder, smiling more, and constantly checking their progress. Trips are great motivators that give specific, short-term goals for employees to work toward.

Create Amazing, Effective Staff Incentives

Studies show incentives are most effective when they follow quarterly, rather than annual, goals. Employees have an easier time hitting goals that must be reached in ninety days than they do hitting goals that are 365 days in the future.

Every incentive should include easily measurable activities, and every employee should know how the goal relates to their role. Incentives can be based on team or individual performances. My advisors usually offer a combo.

The funny thing about the right incentives is that they create chatter outside of your company. Not long ago, my wife and I were enjoying a night out when we started a conversation with a couple sitting next to us. When they heard I work for Advisors Excel, they said, "That's a great company. That's the one that takes employees on a trip every year, right?"

If, instead of taking us on a trip, Advisors Excel, gave every employee a five percent raise, would that couple even know about us? I bet not.

Become the Company Everyone Wants to Work For

Do stuff for staff that 99 percent of other companies fail to do and you'll have an incredible culture.

Do stuff for staff that 99 percent of other companies fail to do and you'll have an incredible culture.

While you're focusing on those big incentives, don't forget the little things. A 2014 TINYpulse study titled, "The 7 Key Trends Impacting Today's Workplace," shows most employees are motivated by praise from managers (88 percent of those polled) and working in a fun environment (90 percent of those polled). The good news is, both are completely under your control.

For some people, this comes naturally. Others have to work at it. Take time each week to acknowledge employees positively. Employees who feel appreciated, like their work is valued, and that someone (you) notices their efforts, are much more productive than those who do not get similar feedback from an employer.

If you want to show your appreciation, you will find ways to do it. One of my advisors sent a thank you card to an employee's spouse, thanking the spouse for supporting the employee at home so she could help them through a few tough weeks. He included a gift card to a nice restaurant so the two could enjoy dinner. The gesture made the employee feel more appreciated for the work she put in than any direct praise my advisor could have given.

Praise can and should be a team effort. Take the whole team to lunch after a big win, or give staff a few extra hours of personal time on a Friday. Try what one of my top advisors does and take the whole team to lunch every time there's a birthday. Not only does everyone get a free meal, the birthday boy or girl clocks out after lunch.

Another often-missed way to develop a winning culture is by creating a culture where employees are constantly learning new things. The best employees feel unfulfilled the minute they're no longer learning or growing. You can and should be an active participant in this growth. Have each staff member report back to you within the next week regarding one area of professional development they're interested in. This could be anything from mastering Excel to increasing their public speaking skills. Once you agree on areas that will benefit your staff and your practice, have each employee find reasonably priced online or in-person trainings to attend and cover the tab. For maximum return on your investment, have staff summarize key takeaways and—if applicable—share them with the rest of the team.

Some advisors hire speakers or trainers every quarter to talk to staff about a specific topic. One of my advisors brought in a former Ritz-Carlton employee to teach his staff about providing a five-star service. Another took his entire staff to a Tony Robbins seminar. They loved it, they learned a lot, they bonded and, even though a year has gone by, they're still talking about the experience.

Another advisor hosts a book club. He has each employee read a book each month. They highlight the best parts, and the highlights are summarized and talked about with staff in relation to the company. This is a brilliant way of running a book club. Instead of reading only a few books a year, everyone gets lessons from many books.

Many advisors take staff on retreats at the beginning or end of each year to discuss upcoming goals or previous production. For many producers, November and December are the perfect time to shut down the office for a day, find a great off-site location, and connect with their teams regarding vision and the strategies they plan to implement in the coming year.

Steve Jobs was a huge fan of this strategy and took his top 100 employees on a retreat every year. Even a one- or two-day company-wide retreat that focuses on growing the business strengthens relationships and leaves staff feeling confident they have a say in the decision-making process.

One of my best advisor's top priorities had nothing to do with production. He wanted to provide a work culture that fulfilled his staff. He wanted to run a business his team enjoyed coming to everyday. He wanted them to feel heard and respected. He wanted to expand their knowledge, and he wanted them to understand the difference they made to clients. He achieved that goal and, as a result, nailed every other one he had, too.

Protect Your Practice

It's one thing to develop a good team; it's another to leave yourself open to disaster in the event one of those team members leaves. It's not a pleasant topic, but every advisor must protect themselves and their practice. I've seen top producers who have spent years, even decades, building their practices, only to hit a few dangerous potholes that have derailed their business.

If you poll a room of financial professionals about the most imminent threats to their businesses, they'll say competition, seminar saturation, interest rates, unattractive products, or industry regulations. Many of these are threats, but none are as risky as a key member leaving your team.

We might puff our chests and spout some mantra about our teams being bigger than any one key member. There's some truth to this, but don't underestimate the impact a key team member unexpectedly leaving can have on your practice and livelihood if you are not properly prepared and protected.

One of my producers recently experienced this when his key operations person left for another opportunity. His leaving impacted every aspect of the business and led to a 30 percent decline in production. Not only was production down, the absence put a huge strain on remaining staff. Instead of focusing on his core activities, my advisor spent all his time and energy trying to pick up the extra slack. Guess how much that one person leaving cost my advisor? Hundreds of thousands of dollars. My advisor couldn't keep up with the normal pace of business. Instead, he was focused on fixing a problem and making up for losses.

Top advisors protect their practice at all times. They have detailed operations manuals that explain every common process used by their team members. These manuals include everything including how to answer phones, greet clients, host events, enter client records, go through the sales process, and process business. Your manual doesn't have to be a 500-page, hard-bound, IRS-looking thing. It can be a basic three-ring binder, but it must cover everything so that if any employee leaves or is absent for an extended period of time, another member of the team can easily step in and pick up where the other employee left off.

Top advisors protect their practice at all times.

Top advisors make sure every single task in the office can be completed by more than one person. There's nothing worse than having a team member try to reinvent a process that was perfected by another employee. Cross train your employees. Do not put yourself in a situation where a vacation or maternity leave bottlenecks the office.

Naturally, throughout the life of your business, employees will leave. Prevent them from taking clients with them by making associate advisors, and ensure all operational support staff sign non-solicit agreements when they're hired. A local attorney can help draft an appropriate non-solicit agreement that adheres to state laws. These agreements are easy to have signed up front, but can be hard to have signed later on. Get this out of the way in the beginning. The last thing you want is to create operations staff and future advisors for your competition.

It takes years to build a business, but only a second to turn it upside down. You spend the majority of your days helping clients protect what they've built. Be sure to protect yourself.

Chapter 26: Develop a Winning Culture

Be the company that everybody wants to work for by:

1) Challenging your staff to improve, and create ways to give them ongoing education

2) Giving incentives that will motivate the whole team

3) Protecting your practice at all times by cross-training employees and creating an operations manual

27

CREATE
RAVING FANS

"One customer well taken care of could be more
valuable than $10,000 worth of advertising."

—*Jim Rohn*

Service falls into one of two categories: Reactive or proactive.
Reactive service is self-explanatory. It occurs anytime
you or your team reacts to a client's need or problem. When
a client calls the office and needs help with anything, the response
is reactive because you're reacting to their request. For reactive service, clients expect a live person. Leaving a voicemail and getting
a call back at the advisor's convenience is prehistoric. Successful businesses have live responders that are well trained, professional, and smiling.

Every interaction a client has with your team is a reflection of
your company. Cover the phones and make sure whoever answers
is friendly and leaves a great first impression. One of my advisors
actually calls this person his Director of First Impressions.

Remember, speed builds trust, so if a client needs something
back by the end of the day, get it to them within minutes. Speedy
service confirms to the client that they're working with the right
team. Clients can't stand delays, and when they're made to wait,
they question their importance. If they continually experience
delays, it's death by 1,000 cuts and they'll leave. Invest more in back

office reactive services than you think you need to so every client has a great experience with ongoing service needs.

Proactive service is when you and your team initiate contact with clients. You've been thinking about them, you want to help, and so you reach out. Proactive service is an opportunity to get a win with the client. For example, say a client needs to take Required Minimum Distributions (RMDs) out of their IRA. Your team calls to remind the client they need to do this and offers to help if needed.

Once, we had an advisor who literally had a key employee call and check in with his clients every month. They would ask the clients how they were doing, if they needed help with anything, or if there were any changes they needed to be aware of. The employee always tried to add value and quickly developed great relationships with the clients.

> Communicating with clients both before there's a problem and while a problem is occurring is critical because the number one reason clients leave advisors isn't performance. It's lack of communication.

When there was a little market turmoil, my advisors had their teams proactively stay in touch with their clients. They checked in with each client and let them know what was going on, talking to them until they felt 100 percent comfortable with the situation. This was a huge win for my advisors. They gained a great deal of respect from their clients, who were used to the 99 percent of advisors who hide behind their desk hoping clients don't call during this type of crisis. Instead of hiding, my advisors looked at the situation as an opportunity to make sure clients were educated and comfortable. They also reminded them to set up additional protections in their plans where needed. It worked beautifully.

When it comes to offering great service for your clients, the sky is the limit. Yes, you need to react to their needs, but don't stop there. Be proactive, and do as much as you can for them.

Communicate or You're Fired

Communicating with clients both before there's a problem and while a problem is occurring is critical because the number one reason clients leave advisors isn't performance. It's lack of communication.

In fact, a 2013 *Financial Advisor*[1] magazine survey asked 1,375 advisors to select the top three reasons clients fire advisors. Seventy-two percent of respondents said, "failure to communicate on a timely basis." So advisors spend all this time talking to clients at the beginning, do all the work to get them in the door, and then fail to communicate? It's a terrible reality, but one that's easy to fix.

The more you communicate with your clients, the more satisfied they will be, but it's important to note the communication doesn't have to be one-on-one time with you. Build systems in your business where you and staff communicate with clients through email, newsletters, phone calls, letters, events, and educational opportunities. Start by launching an e-newsletter, hard copy newsletter, and an occasional update letter.

> The more you communicate with your clients, the more satisfied they will be.

1 http://www.fa-mag.com/news/top-5-reasons-why-clients-fire-advisors-16238. html?section=43

As you grow and add clients, seeing each face-to-face every quarter will become impossible. Because face time is so valuable, start seeing people in a group setting where thirty clients can be seen at a time. If you have thirty clients and typically see each for an hour, a one-hour face-to-face group meeting for those thirty clients saves thirty hours. Developing these systems establishes your business as a true business rather than a one-man or one-woman show. It also allows you to oversee clients while maintaining plenty of free time for continued growth.

Enjoy a 98 Percent Retention Rate

In 2014, practice management software and data services company, PriceMetrix, released a client retention study[2]. It showed that during the two-year "honeymoon" period of an advisor/client relationship, 95 percent of clients stayed with their advisor. In years two through four, however, retention dramatically dipped to 75 percent.

Advisors in the top ninetieth percentile enjoy 98 percent overall retention rates. Those in the tenth percentile have an 84 percent overall retention rate.

Just like relationships with your spouse, kids, or friends, your bond with clients deepens when you spend face time with them. Think about it. How hard is it to switch P&C insurers when you can make the switch online for a savings of 15 percent? Conversely, how hard is it to switch barbers when you've seen them once every three weeks for the last fifteen years?

Simply put, face time matters in our business, and it can't happen less than three to four times a year. Most producers see their clients for annual reviews, but there's dozens of other ways to see your clients throughout the year.

One of my top advisors in the south has a nice educational center in his office where he hosts a monthly financial series for existing clients and their friends. For the small price of invitations and refreshments, he gives clients twelve face-to-face opportunities

---

2 http://www.forbes.com/sites/advisor/2014/01/16/the-keys-to-client-retention/

a year. He outlines topics beforehand and asks clients to choose which are of the most interest. His clients love it. Not only are the clients starved for education, these opportunities fill a need. For the advisor, it's awesome because it only takes an hour of his time to see thirty clients. It doesn't matter if you don't have an education center in your office either. This advisor started hosting these sessions in a restaurant. There's no excuse not to maximize the amount of face time you have with clients.

> ## Simply put, face time matters in our business, and it can't happen less than three to four times a year.

Another top producer hosts a client event at a major league ballpark each summer for clients and their guests. With shuttles, catered food, and an air-conditioned suite, it's become one of his clients' most talked about and highly anticipated summer outings.

Other advisors host wine tastings, summer barbecues that include kids and grandkids, movie premiers, fundraisers, cooking parties, pitch and putts, murder mystery parties, and retirement parties. The list goes on and on. Regardless of which event you choose, each face-to-face meeting with a client leaves an impression on clients and guests that will never be duplicated by another advisor.

If you set up a system of great, personal, ongoing communication, clients won't get the two-year itch and hop advisors.

It's also really important that you not only build a relationship with your client, but also build a relationship with their spouse and children. Say you build a relationship with your client, but not his wife. When your client dies, what happens? Studies reveal that

70 percent[3] of the time a client passes on, their widow finds a new advisor. You work so hard to retain your client and all of a sudden, all of the planning and the relationship you built with that client no longer matters.

You've got to be involved with the children of your clients as well. Did you know that 66 percent[4] of children fire their parents' advisor? More often than not, the children don't know their parents advisor and if they do know them, they don't know them well. It's no wonder this happens, which means year over year, you will lose business due to this happening. What's worse, studies show that 70 percent of wealth is destroyed by the second generation and 90 percent is gone by the third generation. Many times when the kids gain an inheritance, they split the money up and do what they see fit. You've guided their parents financial life along the way, and I would guess you could bring a lot of value to the kids as well in order to help them protect what your client has worked so hard to save. In order for this to happen, the beneficiaries have to know you, and you've got to know them.

I've seen advisors do this a number of ways. You can extend the great service you provide to each survivor. Maybe, with your client's permission, you send a handwritten card to your client's children letting them know that you've been working with their parents. If they ever need anything, just let you know. Maybe you add the kids to your newsletter. Maybe you invite them to an annual client appreciation event or your educational events. I actually had one advisor host a big Hawaiian luau where he invited his clients and their families. Another one did a big summer barbeque where she invited the family. She even organized some entertainment for the kids and encouraged them to bring their grandkids.

Whatever you do, get to know your client's children. Not only will you be at the forefront of their mind when their situation

---

3 http://www.investopedia.com/articles/financial-advisors/011615/why-do-widows-leave-their-advisors.asp
4 http://www.investmentnews.com/article/20150713/FEATURE/150719999/the-great-wealth-transfer-is-coming-putting-advisers-at-risk

changes, you never know when they might need your services, too. Think about it. If you have a client in his eighties, how old are his kids? Fifty? Sixty? Just about the age when they might be looking for a financial advisor, too.

The point is, you don't want to be a complete stranger to beneficiaries; you want them to know who you are and that you care.

Chapter 27: Create Raving Fans

Don't let a lack of communication with clients affect your business. Ask yourself:

1) What can I do today, next week, and next month to provide proactive service to my clients while also improving my reactive service?

2) How can I build systems within my practice to see my clients three to four times per year minimum?

3) How can I build a relationship with my clients' beneficiaries?

28

DEVELOP A PERSONALIZED, POSITIVE, IMPACT CULTURE

"I can't outspend the large financial institutions, but I can out experience them."

— *Elite Advisor, OH*

Now that you have great service and a great team, how can you wow your clients? The wow factor is what you, your business, and your employees should strive for.

Once you've made an effort to overcommunicate with clients and build a culture of great service, make sure every person in the office realizes that every interaction they have is an opportunity to make someone's day. Everyone should walk into the office thinking, "How can I create the ultimate client experience at every opportunity?" Everything you do is about creating personalized, positive impact (PPI).

Set Yourself Miles Ahead of the Competition

Think of it like this. Imagine you're on your way to see your accountant whom you haven't seen for a while. You have an appointment and hope she will remember you. As you pull into the parking lot, you see a parking spot with your name on it—a pleasant surprise. You pull in and walk into the office. The first person you meet—who you've never met before—welcomes you by your first name, hands you a nice professional drink menu, and says, "Would you like an ice tea with a lemon like usual, or would you like to pick a drink from the menu?"

Confused, but flattered by the familiarity, you ask for your usual, sit on a nice comfy chair, and see your name and picture on a welcome sign that says, "Welcome to the office Mr. Jones."

How would this make you feel? Would you look forward to returning to that office? Would you feel important? Would you be confident that you're in good hands?

Personalized, positive, impact makes clients feel like they're part of a personal service. It makes them feel good, it boosts their confidence, and it builds loyalty. It also sets advisors apart from competitors—even the big ones.

As one of my top advisors said, "I can't outspend the large financial institutions, but I can out experience them."

How to Develop Your PPI Culture

There are many ways to develop your PPI culture. Train your team to constantly look for ways to make a client's day with every interaction. Note what your clients like to drink when they come in, and when they return to your office, put their names on a board so they feel welcome.

Keep a database of personalized information, and return to that database frequently to find ways you can provide random acts of kindness for your clients. Your team's job should be to constantly find ways to make a client's day and therefore randomly surprise them. Maybe Mrs. Jones recently mentioned the birth of a new grandchild. What a great opportunity to send a card and baby gift.

If Mr. Peterson is sick, send a care package, and let him know you hope he feels better soon.

Train your team to constantly look for ways to make your client's day with every interaction.

One of my advisors had a client whose grandchild was recognized in the newspaper. A staff member framed the article with a sweet note and sent it to her client. Once you're staff starts doing this, they'll start hearing from happy clients. The feeling that comes from that is addicting. Your staff will want to do this over and over. One advisor I work with actually gives each staff member a monthly budget for this cause. At the end of each month, they have a team meeting and each person shares the random act of kindness they did. The team then votes on the best one and the winner gets to leave on the last Friday of the month at noon. Think about it. This advisor has created a culture where his staff members are actually competing to see who can make their clients feel the most special.

Your team has multiple client interactions every year. Each is an opportunity to personalize their experience and make them feel good. For example, one of my top advisors sends every client who loses a spouse wind chimes to help remember them by. Another, for his clients' milestone birthdays, sends a CD of the top songs that played the year a client turned sixteen. Instead of sending a birthday card like everyone else, one of my advisors sends clients a birthday cake to share with their family.

Make sure all of the little touches come from a person within your office as well, not just the company. Again, we want these to be personal, and sending gifts from a company generically isn't personal at all. The clients won't know who to thank either. Put this process into place, get the team on board, and before long, you won't have to check in with clients from month to month. They will be calling you instead, thanking you for the card, gifts, or cake.

These efforts will help manufacture a positive monthly call-in from your clients and will solidify client loyalty. They will also reinforce your mission and motivate staff. In fact, every time someone in your office succeeds with a personalized, positive impact touch, share it with your entire staff. Show them the difference you're making.

Personalized, positive impact is one of the most effective, fun ways to interact with clients. It greatly enhances the client experience and overrides the old philosophy of just getting by. Personalized, positive impact is the culture you want to create. It's proactive and keeps the lines of communication open, which is a critical element in retaining lifelong client relationships.

How to Let Clients Go While Leaving a Great Impression

It's sobering, but every relationship ends. It happens in our personal lives. It happens in business. At some point, a client may decide to leave you for another advisor or to manage their own investments. Top advisors know this happens from time to time. The idea is to avoid burning bridges and commit to taking the high road with clients no matter what. This attitude will differentiate you from other advisors. Often times, it will also create fantastic opportunities.

Sometimes clients leave without saying a word and just hope they never run into their advisor again. Other times, they feel they owe it to the advisor to discuss the move in person. Regardless, it's rare that an advisor takes the departure well.

I'm sure you've experienced instances when the advisor getting left behind gets ugly and makes the client feel bad about the decision. They back up the guilt truck, throw dirt all over the client's decision, and smear the new advisor—you—in mud.

Here's the deal. It doesn't matter how much time the client spent with another advisor or what that advisor did for them. The last impression that advisor leaves with that client matters most. When advisors get ugly, the impression is always bad, and they permanently burn a bridge.

One out of five clients leaves within the first three years of working with an advisor. Since we know clients are going to leave, let them leave thinking, "If this new opportunity isn't what I think it is, I'm going back to the other advisor. He's a great guy."

As one of my top advisors says, "The last impression is a lasting impression."

Take the emotion out of the exit. If the client says they're changing, understand and address each reason for the departure the best you can. More often than not, once you address each reason, the client will stay. However, if they've made up their mind and the relationship is done, take the high road. Genuinely let them know how grateful you are for the relationship, that you totally respect their decision and want what is best for them whether they do business with you or someone else. Wish them nothing but success. Let them know if the change doesn't work, you would be thrilled to hear from them again and help in whatever way possible.

We have talked about having an incredible culture and doing everything you can to help clients. Even when things don't go your way, go above and beyond for your clients. One of my top advisors actually sends a handwritten thank-you card when a client decides to leave them. He lets them know how much he's enjoyed the relationship, and he appreciates their letting him and his team serve them over the years. And by the way, if anything changes where they can help, they are only a phone call away.

If things don't go the way the client thought they would, or the honeymoon period ends and they find themselves neglected by the new advisor, do you think that client will hesitate to call the old advisor back? No, and it's no surprise clients often come running right back to him as time passes. So many advisors miss opportunities like this because they burn the bridge on the exit.

How you react to the inevitability of failure defines you. Leave every relationship on a positive note. You never know what life has in store, who you'll meet, or when someone might need you.

But if you take care of your team and develop a PPI structure that constantly and consistently creates an exceptional experience for clients, you will have a business structure that fosters long-term relationships and maximizes productivity.

How you react to the inevitability of failure defines you.

Chapter 28: Develop a Personalized, Positive, Impact Culture

Use personalized, positive impact in your office by:

1) Creating a database of your clients' preferences

2) Having everybody in your office stay on the constant lookout for ways to make a client's day

3) No matter what, always taking the high road with clients and never burning a bridge

29

IMPROVE YOUR IMAGE

"Image is everything. You don't spare any expense to create the right image. And word of mouth is critical. Once you get a good reputation, momentum will carry you."

— *Haruki Murakami*

Here's a horror story. I visited an advisor and his receptionist. She is the first touchpoint for clients, but that day she looked like she'd been clubbing. Her clothes were flashy and revealing, and she was wearing way too much makeup for an office environment. Her appearance wouldn't put any client at ease.

In addition to a poor first in-person impression, this advisor's web presence and the materials he sent to clients were unprofessional.

Make Sure Your Office Strengthens Your Position with Your Client

Nothing about your practice should scream amateur. Everything you project has to explain exactly what your practice is about. Everything you do has to be top-notch. Everything functions to increase your credibility with the client. When the clients see you, read your materials, or walk into the office, they have to think, "I made a great decision going with this advisor."

Think about your office for a minute. What feeling do you want clients to get when they walk in for the first time? Does your company look like a million-dollar company? Does your office project success? What should the client expect based on what they see?

If your office doesn't wow clients and leave them confident that they're in the right hands, renovate. Update your office so it projects an image attractive to your clients. Have an office that's so great, one you're so proud of, that clients ask for a tour.

The type of client you work with will affect how you design your office. When you look at your office, think like a client. If you offer food or drink, have nice company-branded coasters for clients to put them on. Place high-caliber marketing materials on lobby tables, and have your welcome video looping on the TV. Put your clients at ease, and let them get to know you while they wait. Think about every detail from the client's perspective. A Styrofoam coffee cup sends a very different message then a glass mug with the company logo. Each detail of your office says something about you. The flowerpot in the corner? That's you. The painting behind the receptionist's desk? Also you. Think about the messages each send. A dead plant sends off a message of negligence. Don't work with us. We don't even pay attention to our plants. A calming, neutral, abstract, or landscape painting will put clients at ease. Picasso's *Guernica* will not.

If you don't have a good grasp on your office image, have a secret shopper—a friend or acquaintance—walk through your office and give honest impressions and feedback. Take that feedback and use it in renovations. Maybe you work with an interior designer to perfect your office image, maybe you don't. Either way, office upgrades work.

Three advisors I work with upgraded their offices with phenomenal results. A couple needed more room, so they moved to bigger offices. One upgraded his current office by bringing in professional designers. The new office design had such an impact on client perception, it paid for itself. It gave the office more credibility and helped the advisor stand out from competition.

The first impression a client has of your company determines whether they want to work with you. Everything you project must scream successful company.

The first impression a client has of your company determines whether they want to work with you. Everything you project must scream successful company.

Remember that you're competing with thousands of advisors. If a $5 million client walked into a room with you and 100 other advisors, would they choose you? Is there anything about your practice that stands out?

If your answer is no, pay attention because this industry won't be getting less competitive any time soon. You have to do everything you can to differentiate yourself from competitors.

8 Ways to Upgrade Your Image Today

1. Get an email address that links to your company domain.
2. Develop a high-end company site that has a clean, simple design, easy navigation, intriguing bios under the About Us section, well edited content, and several videos.
3. Add great images on that site by hiring a professional photographer.
4. Create a strong identity kit of marketing materials. This may include business cards, letterhead, envelopes, greeting cards, presentation folders, and banner stands.

5. Create a professional, two-to-three minute introductory video that explains your why. Use the video on your site, loop it through your lobby TVs, burn it to discs, and send it to high-net-worth referrals.

6. Create bounce-back videos, or personal videos that go to clients via email during the sales process.

7. Leverage a series of high-end deliverables in your calls to action. Well-written, professionally designed, high-end deliverables discussing a number of topics provide that support, demonstrate your firm's professionalism, and help educate clients before they meet with you.

8. Write a book about something you know well. Writing a book makes you an authority on a subject, increases your credibility, and makes you stand out from competitors.

While they may seem small, each of these differentiators is important to shaping your overall image. At the end of the day, when a client is deciding between you and ten other advisors, image is everything.

Chapter 29: Improve Your Image

If image is everything, make sure you're projecting the right one.

1) Is your office giving the image of a successful company? Consider hiring an interior decorator or upgrading it if not

2) Do your collateral materials fit the image of your office?

3) Hire a secret shopper to test drive your office and give you honest feedback on how you can improve your image

30

ACT CHARITABLY

"No person was ever honored for what he received. Honor has been rewarded for what he gave."

— *Calvin Coolidge*

Just like this business shouldn't just be about money for you personally, it shouldn't just be about money for your business either. It should be about helping people and making a difference. A way to do this is through philanthropy.

With the rise of social media, social enterprises, and crowdfunding, it's no longer enough to just add value with products and services. To retain employees and clients, you have to show you have substance. Yes, clients need to know you can make and manage money, but more importantly, they need to know that you are a reputable, caring business.

Consumers crave a deeper connection with businesses, which is why they friend or like businesses on Facebook, follow them on Twitter, sign up for email newsletters, and read company blogs. They want more of you. They also want to know you stand for something. They need to see your substance.

Take TOM's shoes and Warby Parker. For every pair of shoes purchased, TOM's gives a pair of shoes to a child in need. Warby Parker does something similar with glasses. For every pair of glasses purchased, the company provides a pair to someone in need. Both companies have a great reputation among consumers. They provide a good product, but they also work closely with charities. Consumers know they stand for something other than profit.

Be Better Than 89 Percent of Advisors

All other things being equal, a 2013 Cone Communications Social Impact Study[1] shows 89 percent of US consumers are likely to switch brands to ones associated with a cause. What are you waiting for? Start giving.

While you may not be able to donate a large portion of your earnings to charity the way some larger corporations do, as a small business owner you can show clients there's more to your practice than money. Free social media sites such as Facebook and Twitter will tell you what your clients care about. Listen to those conversations, find out where your clients are volunteering, and what causes they get behind, and show your support.

Solidify a Feeling of Community

Many charities need physical help more than they need money. Instead of hosting a fundraiser, set aside a full workday for you, your employees, and your clients to do some hands-on charity work. Take a day as a team and fill backpacks for underserved kids who are going back to school, or spend a day helping your local rescue mission or children's hospital. Set a tangible goal for your clients or team to hit. Maybe it's to feed 100 families, or impact twenty children, or give fifty Christmas gifts. If you don't identify with a charity as an organization, give employees a day off to volunteer at their own personal favorite charity.

Ultimately, hosting a charitable event allows your clients to connect with you in completely different way. It allows them to experience your values and see how much you truly care. It also solidifies

---

1 http://www.causemarketingforum.com/site/apps/nlnet/content2.aspx?c=bkLUKc OTLkK4E&b=6430205&ct=13344211&notoc=1

a feeling of community with your firm, lets the community know you're around to stay, and gives your clients a chance to give back, too.

To weave the charity into your practice, promote it at an upcoming client event and explain why you're committed to making a difference. Let clients know you'll match all donations made to that charity within the next year to a certain cap. Give anyone who donates a raffle ticket and draw a fun prize at the end of the event. If one of your clients donates more than $100, give them a badge or a blinking light that makes them stand out and feel special.

Or, if you like an existing charity event, piggyback on it. One of my top advisors cuts a check and sponsors a refreshment tent at the city's annual Relay for Life walk. Prior to the event, he mails existing clients and ask them to participate. He also asks for the names of family members who have been impacted by breast cancer. On the day of the event, not only does he have a huge branded tent with water bottles and treats bearing his logo, but hundreds of his clients walk also around a track in branded t-shirts that include the name of family members who are cancer survivors. It's an incredible way to honor his clients and their loved ones while also supporting the larger cause.

Whichever charity you choose, get the word out about your charitable activities not only to the public through social media, but also to clients and staff. Display photos of your charitable work in prominent places throughout your office, and include them in your next client newsletter. If you're so inclined, invite media to the charity event. Media love to cover fundraisers, and their presence allows for free advertising. Plus, the presence of media will impress your clients and make them feel like they are part of something big and important.

Secure a Lasting Spot in Your Clients' Hearts and Lives

Sometimes advisors worry they won't be able to get their clients to participate in these events. If that's the case, send clients a survey with the top three charities you want to support, tell them your plans, and ask them to vote. Once they vote, they're emotionally invested. When you ask them to participate in the fundraiser or the volunteer day, they will be much more likely to jump on board.

If done correctly, charitable work makes a huge impact on clients. It reaches their hearts instead of their wallets and says you're much more than just a financial advisor.

If done correctly, charitable work makes a huge impact on clients. It reaches their hearts instead of their wallets and says you're much more than just a financial advisor.

Chapter 30: Act Charitably

Eighty-nine percent of US consumers are likely to switch brands to ones associated with a cause, so what are you waiting for?

1) Find a cause your clients care about

2) Partner with a charity that supports that cause

3) Commit to supporting that charity at an upcoming client event, and encourage clients to get involved

31

CLONE YOUR CLIENTS

"We constantly market to the cold masses while standing on a diamond field: our current clients."

— Darren Hardy

Now that you've built a business that takes great care of your clients, and you know how to show them an incredible experience with every interaction, your clients will take great care of you as well. You've built a referable business, which means your clients will actually clone themselves by bringing you more people just like them. But once you have this culture built, you've got to make it easy for your clients to refer their friends to you.

Get Clients to Fill Your Schedule

Sometimes in life you don't get what you want, you get what you deserve. When it comes to referrals, I believe this is true. If you are getting referrals, you probably deserve them. If you are not, you probably don't.

So many advisors talk about the best way to generate referrals. How do they ask existing clients for them? What's the best way to get them? Here's a tip: don't ask for referrals at all. Instead, create incredible opportunities where existing clients would like to bring friends.

Remember, the key to generating referrals is creating a referable business that incorporates every single thing we've discussed up to this point. Always start by doing the right thing for your clients. Give them a great experience. If you do that, your business will reward you through referrals.

The Easiest Way to Get Limitless Referrals

Advisors who have great referral businesses have such a high-quality culture that their clients become raving fans and brag to friends about the great job they're doing. This, of course, makes it really easy for them to refer friends to you.

If you don't provide a great service for clients, no matter how nicely you ask, you won't get referrals. Your business should be designed to always go over the top for your clients. The better you do that, the more referrals you will get.

The most profitable business you can have is a referral-based business. Think about it. Not a single marketing dollar is spent when a client refers a friend to you. In addition, the chance of the referred client being a good client is much higher than if the new client came from public marketing efforts. Why? They were referred to you by one of your clients.

I've spent a lot of time breaking down advisors' closing ratios. A prospect that started as a referral is much more likely to become a client than a prospect gained through public marketing efforts. If referral business is more profitable, easier, and more enjoyable, why not put energy and effort into that funnel of your business?

Clone Your Favorite Clients

We all have a special spot in our hearts for certain clients. They share our values, they treat our staff well, they're easy to work with—whatever the reasons—and we wish we had ten more just like them. Every advisor's dream is to have more high-quality referrals from these existing clients.

Top advisors have a consistent referral process. They have solid systems for creating experiences that exceed the expectations. They also provide consistent, high-quality work for their clients. They constantly show clients how much they love them and give them ample opportunity to brag to friends about their awesome advisor. Then, they give those well-cared-for clients regular opportunities to refer their friends to them.

The most profitable business you can have is a referral-based business.

One of my female advisors, who is single, felt single women were being underserved in the financial advising industry. This business is fairly male dominated, and this advisor felt single women in particular were not getting the attention or dedication they needed from other advisors. This advisor quickly became passionate about making a difference to this demographic.

As this advisor started talking in greater depth to this market, she realized they generally weren't too interested in Valentine's Day. So what did this advisor do? She scheduled a Valentine's Day luncheon so this group could get together, play games, and enjoy the day.

During the luncheon, the advisor didn't say a single word about business. She showed her guests a great time while also showing how much she cared about and appreciated them. You wouldn't believe the end result: her clients loved it. In fact, they couldn't wait to do the same thing the following year.

The next year, my advisor told these clients they could bring friends. The women were so excited, one even asked if she could have a whole table for her friends. One great event and my advisor had a room of thirty-three referrals. She made her favorite clients feel special, showed them a great time, and they cloned themselves. She repeated this year after year, and as you can imagine, this one idea ended up creating a ton of great referrals for her business.

The Referral-Generating, Client-Cloning Strategy

Another great way to get referrals is what one of my advisors calls his "client cloning" strategy.

Try this. Have your staff identify the birthdays of your top ten clients. Find the nearest birthday on the list and let that client know "you just realized somebody has a birthday coming up and you want to do something special for them this year."

Invite them and two of their best friends—their peers—out for a nice dinner. They choose the restaurant, but the evening is on you.

On the birthday evening, enjoy a great dinner, show the client a great time, and get to know their friends personally. Do not talk about business. Before dessert, say how much you enjoyed dinner and their company and excuse yourself because you have to head back a little early. Let them know that whether they want dessert or not, they should order it anyway because it's already paid for. This leaves the client and their friends at the table for another fifteen minutes while you leave. During dessert, guess who will be the topic du jour? You. They'll chat about the nice advisor who took them to a birthday dinner.

Let a couple of days pass. More than likely, your client—or the friend—will call. If you don't hear from either, call your client and thank them for letting you share their special day. Let them know how much you enjoyed their friend's company as well. More than likely, the client will share how much their friends liked you. This is your opportunity.

By the way, one of my top advisors told me you don't ask your best clients for referrals, you ask them for advice on how you can find more people just like them. This is key: everybody loves sharing advice. In this instance, you would ask your client for some advice. Ask them if they think it would be a good idea for you to send their friend a thank-you card, or some information from time to time. They will—of course—encourage this. Get their information and start adding these friends to your marketing lists, seminar mailers, and newsletter.

If you do this ten times over the course of the year, you will meet twenty great potential clients who are similar to your top clients. Imagine getting one referral a year from all of your top clients. Not only will you always have new people to see, they'll be the right people for your business.

Elite advisors go over the top and give their clients an incredible experience consistently. But they also make it easy for their clients to introduce their friends to them.

Marketing   Appointments

Revenue

Clients

Great Experience

You've learned all about marketing, sales, and how to build an incredible team, which gives your clients an incredible experience. The formula for what you've created—if done well—will make it so your clients actually clone themselves, and your business will grow organically. But in order to do this, you've got to give them opportunities— like the ones we've mentioned here—to refer people to you. Be creative, and put energy into creating these types of opportunities for your clients, and watch how big of a difference it will make for your business.

B   O   A   R   D

Chapter 31: Clone Your Clients

If you're ready to increase the referrals you get, make sure you:

1) Have incredible events that clients want to bring friends to

2) Utilize the client-cloning strategy

3) Ask clients for advice instead of referrals

SECTION 4:
MASTER OPERATIONS
SUMMARY

S uccess is as much about what you don't do as it is what you do. Learn to delegate, develop a structure that protects your time, and prioritize your activities. Do not fall victim to The Advisor Curse where you try to do everything yourself. Million-dollar advisors are master delegators who fill their calendars with core activities—namely, seeing clients—and let staff get on with their own core activities.

Well-trained staff will grow your business while you're out of the office, but they will need some of your time, so schedule staff catch-ups into your daily calendar, and hire people who support your culture. Be slow and meticulous in your hiring process.

Use personality tests to determine how each person works and communicates so teamwork becomes seamless. If someone doesn't work out, let them go immediately, and part ways on good terms. Treat staff like you would your best customers. Get them to buy into your vision, provide clear expectations, give them positive feedback and great benefits, and frequently offer training opportunities. Understand that every service you offer is either reactive or proactive. Reactive services should be topnotch and responded to quickly. Proactive actions are an opportunity to provide excellent service and exceed client expectations.

The number one reason clients leave is lack of communication. Make sure you see clients at least three to four times a year. Let clients know that you *and* your team are there for them and that it's a team effort. Introduce clients to your key team members immediately so they feel comfortable working with them. This frees you to work on your core activities. Bring personalized, positive impact to clients at every opportunity.

Your office, staff, and personal appearance must mirror the image you hope clients have of your business. Always strive to improve your image with clients whether it's upgrading your office, enhancing the quality of your collateral materials, or improving your website. Find charities that your clients care about and support them. Donating time and money to great causes humanizes your business thereby separating you from the competition. Everything we've learned about so far will help you build a referral-based business. But you have to make it easy for clients to refer people to you in order to capitalize on it.

SUMMARY

Section 4: Master Operations

Top Three GO Elite Actions to Master Operations:

1) Hire, train, and treat your team like you would your number one client

2) Project an image to clients that supports the outstanding service you will provide

3) Build a referral-based business by constantly exceeding client expectations and making it easy for clients to refer friends to you

95 WAYS TO GO ELITE

"Success without fulfillment is failure."
— *Tony Robbins*

For me, the greatest professional rush is not watching my own career advance, but helping my advisors succeed, which is why I've developed the GO Elite Advisor Action Plan. In ninety-five easy steps, you can take every lesson learned in this book and accelerate your business.

Success means different things to different people. Sometimes, I'll see an advisor who is doing really well financially only to realize he hasn't taken a vacation in fifteen years. Other times, I'll see an advisor who some may consider a small fish run the ultimate business, one that rewards him with freedom, minimal stress, and a fantastic quality of life.

Some advisors strive to build huge companies. They want a big business that employs hundreds of people and serves thousands of clients. They want a big machine. Others don't want that at all. Instead, they want a successful business with ten employees or fewer that allows them to work when they want so they're not a slave to their business. Others just want to bring in more assets or revenue.

In this business, success is about achieving the business you want. It's about having a business that blesses your life without *being* your life. One that makes you happier, not one that leaves you miserable.

> In this business, success is about achieving the business you want. It's about having a business that blesses your life without *being* your life.

You and every other advisor out there have the ability to build the business of your dreams. You have what it takes to do more and be better. You have what it takes to mold and shape your business into whatever you want it to be. The opportunities for your business are endless. You can be among the minority of hard-working advisors who have phenomenal success. Be clear in what you want, make sure that driver is fulfilling, and go get it.

For more than ten years, I've worked with thousands of very different advisors who operate very different businesses. I've seen advisors who are great people doing what they love while also enjoying life's greatest luxuries. They know the game isn't about ego or measuring their production against someone else's. These are the advisors who have rewarding businesses that allow them to spend time doing what they love with people they love. These advisors are so past the idea of chasing the next buck, they don't even watch the money roll in. To them, it's meaningless. Their purpose—their motivation—is far greater than money.

One of the greatest offshoots of success is that once you reach a certain level, money matters less. This frees you to make decisions based on what's important to you. I work with advisors who have done so well they actually give away the majority of what they make. Their satisfaction is giving. The rewards of their hard work go to people who need it most.

When money is no longer the object, work also becomes a lot more fun. I know several advisors who show up to work not because they have to, but because they want to. Working with people who show up to work because they want to be there is so much more fun than working with people who show up because they have to. When work becomes fun, productivity increases.

Once, I spoke with a businessman worth hundreds of millions of dollars and asked him why he kept working when clearly there was no longer a need. He said, "Everybody needs achievement in their life."

Very few people embrace this perspective, but it's a powerful position to be in and drastically impacts productivity.

I recently met with an advisor who had been successful for years. One day, he thought, "Another dollar is not going to change my life, I don't have to work another day. Why not just build this business based on what I like doing?"

He changed his business so he only had to meet with three clients a week. He hired a couple of key team members and built a referral-based practice. Any interested referral had to meet him for lunch on Tuesday, Wednesday, or Thursday. That was his schedule. Everything else was taken care of by his rock star staff.

Guess what? This advisor brings in $500,000 a year, doesn't do any marketing, has a business that gives him freedom, and earns a high profit margin. He has no reason to ever quit the business. His business is exactly as he wants it to be.

Too many advisors rate success on assets brought in or revenues. Money is the only driver, but having more money doesn't mean you're better off.

I met a guy a few years back who wrote $40 million a year. Guess what? He kept less than $200,000 in revenue. He put forth all of that time and effort only to keep what advisors who bring in less than a quarter of that business keep. So many people focus on the revenue only to have a terrible business. They have a big mess, less profit, and less freedom. What's the point?

It's fairly easy to grow your business and increase revenue and production. It's a lot harder to grow profitably. Growing in a more controlled manner by gradually decreasing your business's dependence on your physical presence, results in more free time and increased profitability.

A self-sustaining practice is better than a growth practice that drives you crazy. I'd rather you make $1 million a year for ten years, then $3 million in a year, burn out, and start each day with, "I can't wait until I can quit doing this. I can't wait to get out and retire."

The right business puts you in control. It has you starting each day excited and ready to go. It's a business you look forward to being in, not one you can't wait to get out of.

It's even worse to see an enormously successful advisor—someone everyone else celebrates as the ultimate advisor—to find out that internally, the advisor isn't at all successful. Internally, he struggles greatly.

> The right business puts you in
> control. It has you starting each day
> excited and ready to go. It's a business
> you look forward to being in, not
> one you can't wait to get out of.

This type of advisor increases their lifestyle proportionately to their business success. Suddenly, they're stuck in a rat race and are no better off than they were when they made half the income.

In 2014, one of my advisors said, "You know, Shawn, I spend every day helping people plan for retirement, but the truth is, I don't have a retirement plan myself."

No matter how much you produce, or how much money you make, you work way too hard not to have something sustainable to show for it. I'm not talking about short-term perks such as the square footage of your home or trips to St. Thomas. I'm talking long-term assets (outside of your business) like the very ones you help your clients with.

Too often after a record-breaking year, advisors reward themselves by quadrupling the size of their house, adding a pool, buying new cars, or blowing out their wardrobe. Before you know it, they're upside down. In some cases, instead of spending too much, they give too little and stop paying taxes. Soon, they have the IRS at their door and the business they thought they had is gone in an instant. They thought the money would never stop because they'd already watched it flow. As true as it may be, this mentality puts an even greater pressure on that advisor to produce more. At a certain point, they have no choice but to maintain business growth or fall apart. This level of financial pressure is a heavy burden that requires that their business be all about the money.

Imagine if clients saw the financial statements and net worth of these advisors. Is there any chance they'd follow their lead? Probably not. Not only does this freewheeling approach to personal financial management bode poorly for clients, it has a massive impact on the advisor. It creates immense amounts of stress, forcing desperate advisors to focus on the revenue as opposed to focusing on helping people. Sadly, I've worked closely with advisors—people I consider friends—who have allowed themselves to feel so much stress and pressure that they have declared bankruptcy or taken their own lives.

These situations are heartbreaking. It's especially difficult for a guy like me, who has looked up to these advisors only to realize I had no idea what was really going on. What is the point of success if it doesn't better your life? The experience available in this business swings from one extreme or the other. You control which way it goes. You set the discipline and structure that determines the direction of your business.

> # What is the point of success if it doesn't better your life?

Think about how incongruent and inconsistent these advisors' lifestyles are to the messages they share with clients. When they tell clients to practice frugality during earning years, live off a budget and save, they should do the same, yet they spend every dollar they make and are careless with their own money. The thing is, when you practice what you preach, you reach a point of abundance, and the entire process from marketing to sales to operations becomes radically different. Why? Because you no longer need the sale. When what you're doing personally enhances your life, it transfers right back to your business. It leads to a better business, better culture, and better experience.

Imagine developing a business where you genuinely don't have to worry about money or the potential revenue on your next case. Imagine a business where money is the last thing you think about. Advisors who reach this point have worked hard and smart and made a series of choices that have allowed their business to bless their life rather than burden it. They have a freedom most advisors do not, are happy, and only continue working because it fulfills them.

One of my top advisors learned a valuable lesson from his clients who are typically moving into retirement. These clients work their entire lives hoping that when they retire, they'll have all the free time in the world. Guess what? When they retire, it isn't as great as they thought it would be.

Because they were nearly addicted to being busy and working, they have no idea what to do with so much time. They started struggling with their relationship with their spouse, who they normally didn't see so much throughout the day. Instead of finding something to do, they spend a lot of time reflecting on their life. They are miserable.

My advisor realized these clients spent too much time focusing on getting out of their industries and retiring and not enough time on developing a professional lifestyle they'd never want to leave. Learning from this, he built a business he truly enjoyed and would therefore never want to leave.

Not only is it unfulfilling to spend time looking back on what you've done, it's unhealthy. Each of us is either growing or dying. Keep growing, but do it at a rate you enjoy. Make it a reality.

Each of us is either growing
or dying. Keep growing, but
do it at a rate you enjoy.

One case, decision, or employee does not determine the trajectory of your career. It's every single little thing that counts. Every little thing you do—every decision you make—determines your destiny in this business. Your business is a reflection of you and the decisions you've made.

You spend so much of your life in your career, build one you enjoy. Rewards should enhance your life rather than tying you to a ball and chain. Follow elite advisors, enter a place where freedom matters over money, and happiness will follow.

After working with thousands of advisors, I am convinced that any advisor can make it. You have what it takes to succeed, but I don't want that success to blindside and disappoint you. Life is much more important than business, and business is much more important than money. You don't want to be one of those advisors who looks back on his career and says, "I wish I hadn't been so focused on my business. I wish I had spent more time with family or developed a business I could leave for a few weeks so I could go on a family vacation."

Advisors with these regrets haven't applied the principles outlined in *Breakthrough* to their practice. They're the advisors who have nothing to talk about but business. What about family? What about the one million other things they could have in their life?

Don't let your practice become a ball and chain. Follow elite advisors and strive for a place where money no longer matters. Get to a point where your business becomes so much more than a money machine.

It's so cool to watch success positively change the trajectory of someone's life. The high point of my professional life is watching an advisor go from just getting by to having an incredible impact on themselves and others.

The good news is, after watching thousands of advisors for the last ten years, I can tell you just about everybody has what it takes to succeed. Little, consistent actions separate those who capitalize on opportunity and those who remain in a state of potential.

Little, consistent actions
separate those who capitalize
on opportunity and those who
remain in a state of potential.

I'm confident that if you implement even 5 percent of the ideas discussed in the GO Elite Advisor Action Plan, you'll see significant growth in your business during the next twelve months. Dig in, work hard, focus on your mission, and master marketing, sales, and operations. When you do, you will have a better business which in turn will allow you to help more people.

I can't wait to see you among the smiling faces of the elite.

YOUR GO ELITE ADVISOR ACTION PLAN

95 Actions That Will Accelerate Your Business

SECTION 1: MASTER THE GAME

Chapter 1: Know What You Want

Paint a clear picture of your ideal business by:

1) Clearly defining what rewards you want from your business

2) Developing a vision around those rewards

3) Sharing that vision with your team

Chapter 2: Separate the Mission from the Commission

Pinpointing the motivation for your goals is the only thing that will get you through those tough moments. Ask yourself:

4) Why am I in this business?

5) Why do I want to grow?

6) What is the real intent of my business?

Chapter 3: Get Impatient
Practice impatience.

7) List five ideas you feel would improve your current business

8) Rank them according to importance

9) Take the first step to implement the best idea within seventy-two hours

Chapter 4: Become a Student of the Game
Learn something from everyone you know.

10) List three things you want to know about or improve in your business

11) List the resources—people, books, websites, blogs— that can lead you to those answers

12) Send an email or call the resources on those lists and start answering those questions

Chapter 5: Take Consistent, Constant Action
Are you setting yourself up for success? Ask yourself the following:

13) Am I putting in enough hours today to get the business I hope to have in the future?

14) Do I know specifically how many people I need to see every day to reach my current goal?

15) Am I seeing enough people every week in order to reach this goal?

SECTION 2: MASTER MARKETING

Chapter 6: Master Your Cash Flow

To make a smart investment in your marketing strategy:

16) Calculate how many appointments each marketing funnel generates

17) Understand how much each appointment is worth and how much revenue each funnel generates

18) Don't put a large percentage of your marketing dollars into branding

Chapter 7: Speak Your Clients' Language

Make the most out of your marketing budget by:

19) Using a survey to profile your ideal client

20) Only marketing what you do best

21) Developing a message that supports your skillset and targets your ideal client

Chapter 8: Know Your Numbers

Want to double your business? Take a look at your numbers.

22) Crunch the numbers for each of your funnels

23) Decide which funnels need more resources, which need improvement, and which should be discontinued

24) Choose one funnel that needs improvement, and develop an action plan for improving that funnel

Chapter 9: Evolve Your Marketing Strategy

Take a look at your funnels and ask yourself the following:

25) How many marketing funnels do I currently use in my business?

26) What new funnels could I add to my practice?

27) Who do I know that uses that funnel currently whom I could learn from?

Chapter 10: Rocket Fuel Your Business

Think about cutting your expenses. Before you do, answer the following:

28) What are my fixed costs?

29) What are my fuel costs?

30) What is one appointment worth to my business?

Chapter 11: Be a Farmer and a Hunter

Don't let a single prospect fall through the cracks.

31) Dig out contact information from prospects who decided not to do business with you

32) Add them to your drip list

33) Stay in touch in case things change, and find ways to bring value to them from time to time

Chapter 12: Understand the Value of an Appointment
Stop wasting time with the wrong prospects and start focusing on spending time with the right ones. Ask yourself:

34) What's the value of my appointments?

35) Which of the three strategies to increase revenue do I want to pursue?

36) How can I change my business model to reach that goal?

Chapter 13: Be Consistent and Persistent
To grow your business, constantly prime the pump by:

37) Committing to consistently marketing year-round

38) Planning your marketing calendar for a full year at a time

39) Refusing to leave your business vulnerable because it's based on one marketing strategy

SECTION 3: MASTER SALES

Chapter 14: Sell to Serve
Next time you go to make a sale, try the following:

40) Get to know the client on a personal level by asking detailed questions that unveil their relationship with money

41) Listen more than you talk

42) Weave the client's story into your solution

Chapter 15: Tell Great Stories

Showing your clients who you are by sharing a personal story will make them remember *and* trust you. Here's how to do it:

43) Use the power of dramatic demonstration and props to add color to the stories you tell

44) Include emotional elements and your motivations in your story

45) Use the power of dramatic demonstration and props to add color to your story

Chapter 16: Believe in What You're Selling

Share your belief with clients by:

46) Preparing for your next appointment by answering the question, "If a client came to me with handful of quotes, what sets me apart from the other advisors?"

47) Mapping out and naming your process

48) Differentiating yourself from competitors by selling your unique process

Chapter 17: Practice Value-Based Selling

The advisor who adds the most value wins.

49) Do you add enough value that your clients would write a check every month for your ongoing services?

50) How can you add more value to your clients so they would actually be willing to pay a premium for your services?

51) Listen to your clients on an ongoing basis and start building systems within your business to be more valuable

Chapter 18: Adopt These Three Steps to Bulletproof the Sale
Nail your sales process by:

52) Setting the right expectations with clients up front

53) Having your client take ownership of the problem

54) Keeping yourself at the forefront of your client's mind after the sale by sending them a series of high-quality communications during your first sixty days together

Chapter 19: Objections Made Easy
Don't let objections control you. Ask yourself:

55) What objections are most common in my sales process?

56) How can I address these objections during my sales process before they're raised?

57) How can I pay better attention to clients during my sales process to understand the motivations behind their objections?

Chapter 20: Seal the Deal Like a Pro
Never forget to ask for the business. Here are three key factors in sealing the deal:

58) Be sincerely convinced your prospects need your help

59) Don't be afraid to ask for the business

60) Do so well that the clients ask you for the business

Chapter 21: Set Realistic Expectations

Avoid setting expectations you can't uphold by asking yourself the following:

61) What expectations do I set for clients and do they align with the service I provide?

62) Which of my expectations—for products and services—are unsustainable?

63) How can I bring the concept of underpromise/overdeliver to my practice?

Chapter 22: Sell More with a Top-Notch Team

The image we think we project isn't always the same as the image we actually project. Test drive your client experience by:

64) Determining whether your staff is *really* trained to sell the experience you would like them to sell

65) Determining whether you're currently serving as a connector for your clients

66) Having a friend test drive your experience so they can report back to you

SECTION 4: MASTER OPERATIONS

Chapter 23: Establish a Team That Helps You Win Big

You need an incredible team to help you reach your goals. Be sure to:

67) Build a great team around you

68) Hire people who can overcompensate for your weaknesses

69) Create a culture where your employees work a ton to protect your time so you can focus on what's most important

Chapter 24: Avoid the Advisor Curse

When it comes to filling your calendar, don't stumble over dollars to pick up pennies.

70) Make more revenue per sale by focusing on filling your calendar exclusively with your highest value work

71) Hire an assistant to do low-value activities so you can focus on doing what you do best

72) Let staff do the things their good at their way—don't micromanage

73) Consider hiring an associate advisor to increase the sales capacity of your business

Chapter 25: Empower Your Team
Great teams build great businesses. Build your team by:

74) Using personality tests to decipher their preferred communication styles

75) Ensuring your hiring process is designed to bring A+ people into your office

76) Developing a meeting structure that creates a more open, positive workplace

77) Always using we instead of I when talking to clients about your business

Chapter 26: Develop a Winning Culture
Be the company everybody wants to work for by:

78) Challenging your staff to improve and create ways to give them ongoing education

79) Giving incentives that will motivate the whole team

80) Protecting your practice at all times by cross-training employees and creating an operations manual

Chapter 27: Create Raving Fans
Don't let a lack of communication with clients affect your business. Ask yourself:

81) What can I do today, next week, and next month to provide proactive service to my clients while also improving my reactive service?

82) How can I build systems within my practice so these proactive communications come from staff, not me?

83) How can I build a relationship with my clients' beneficiaries?

Chapter 28: Develop a Personalized, Positive, Impact Culture

Use personalized, positive impact in your office by:

84) Creating a database of your clients' preferences

85) Having everyone in your office on the constant look-out for ways to make a client's day

86) No matter what, always taking the high road with clients and never burning a bridge

Chapter 29: Improve Your Image

If image is everything, make sure you're project-ing the right one.

87) Is your office giving the image of a successful com-pany? Consider hiring an interior decorator or upgrading it if not

88) Do your collateral materials fit the image of your office?

89) Hire a secret shopper to test drive your office and give you honest feedback on how you can improve your image

Chapter 30: Act Charitably

Eighty-nine percent of United States consumers are likely to switch brands to ones associated with a cause so what are you waiting for?

90) Find a cause your clients care about

91) Partner with a charity that supports that cause

92) Commit to supporting that charity at an upcoming client event, and encourage clients to get involved

Chapter 31: Clone Your Clients

If you're ready to increase the referrals you get, make sure you:

93) Have incredible events that clients want to bring friends to

94) Utilize the client-cloning strategy

95) Ask clients for advice instead of referrals

ABOUT THE AUTHOR

As vice president of advisor development for Advisors Excel, the country's fastest-growing insurance marketing organization, Shawn Sparks works with some of the country's most elite financial advisors. He helps clients earn more than $1.3 billion in sales annually by teaching them to develop businesses that work for them rather than one that owns them. Unlike the average financial advisor who makes $75,320 a year, Shawn's clients earn an average of more than $400,000 a year while working less than forty hours a week. Shawn loves sharing his foundation for success with financial advisors and is adamant that the most successful sales professionals focus on helping people rather than on growing assets. Although he loves basketball and working out, Shawn's favorite pastime is family time. Shawn adores spending time with his wife Aubrey and his two daughters Sadie and AnnMarie. Shawn lives in Lawrence, Kansas.

www.shawnsparks.com

www.the52sparks.com

LET'S STAY CONNECTED

I am surrounded by many of the nation's most elite advisors. We face new challenges and opportunities collectively. Together we work to enhance the potential of all of our success. If you'd like to stay connected with me, there are a number of ways to do it.

WANT A VIDEO LESSON EVERY WEEK?

Subscribe to our 52 Sparks videos:
SHAWNSPARKS.COM/THE-52-SPARKS

Every Sunday morning, receive custom videos, intriguing audio clips, and practical insights and tips from other mega-producers like yourself. I have compiled these resources for your business to help you improve your practice, production, and life.

DO YOU HAVE A QUESTION OR WANT MORE INFORMATION ABOUT SOMETHING IN THE BOOK?

Are you looking to breakthrough your business to the next level? My team will do a 30-minute strategy session with you.

Please email: BREAKTHROUGH@SHAWNSPARKS.COM

For more information about me,
please visit SHAWNSPARKS.COM

CONNECT ON SOCIAL MEDIA:
Twitter: @shawncsparks
Facebook: facebook.com/shawncsparks/

Advisors Excel takes a holistic approach to helping financial professionals build dynamic practices so they are free to create the business and life they want, while helping their clients create their desired retirement lifestyles as well.

For many IMOs and financial institutions, growing your business means increasing your production. That's certainly part of business growth, but if that growth comes at the expense of the other things in your life—time with family, time pursuing your passions, time to give to the causes near and dear to you—what have you actually accomplished?

By providing support for every aspect of the business —marketing, lead generation, product knowledge, case design, business processing, operations, and infrastructure —Advisors Excel allows financial professionals to create the kind of businesses that support the lifestyles they want, and that best support their clients in achieving the lifestyles they desire in retirement.

For more information, visit advisorsexcel.com

Made in the USA
Las Vegas, NV
06 December 2020